The Courtship of Mr. Lincoln

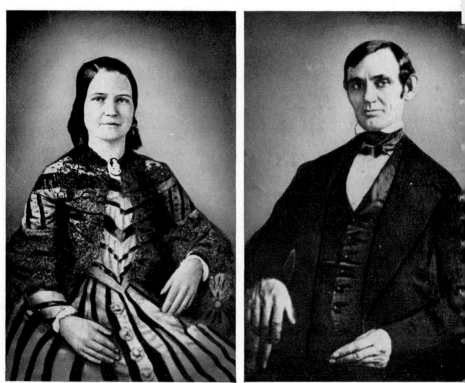

Earliest Known Pictures of Abraham and Mary

This is the closest one can get to the appearance of Miss Todd and the young lawyer who courted her. These companion daguerreotypes were taken, it is now believed, about 1846, four years after their marriage.

The Courtship of
MR. LINCOLN

RUTH PAINTER RANDALL

With Illustrations

Boston • Little, Brown and Company • *Toronto*

Published simultaneously in Canada
by Little, Brown & Company (Canada) Limited

PRINTED IN THE UNITED STATES OF AMERICA

*For Jim
who read the early chapters
of this book — and asked me
to finish it*

Foreword

THIS work was begun while *Mary Lincoln: Biography of a Marriage* was in production. In that book, published early in 1953, I attempted to show by strict historical evidence the falseness of certain prevailing ideas about the Lincoln marriage which had been launched by William H. Herndon, Lincoln's law partner. Herndon in his biography of Lincoln gave an elaborate description of a wedding occasion at which Lincoln as bridegroom failed to appear. Such an occasion has long been discredited by scholars; it was a product of Herndon's vivid imagination and was part of his larger and basic fabrication that the Lincoln-Todd marriage was not a love match. This false premise with the defaulting bridegroom story had for many years colored public thinking about the courtship.

In treating this period in my biography of Mrs. Lincoln I therefore had to combat these distortions of Herndon's and present the romance of Abraham Lincoln and Mary Todd in an unfitting atmosphere of argument and refutation. This was necessary in attempting a definitive biography, yet was anything but desirable as a way in which to relate a great American love story, whose dramatic ele-

ments — broken engagement, family opposition, secret
meetings of the lovers, and a challenge to a duel — out-
strip most works of fiction.

So it was my wish when I finished the life of Mrs. Lincoln to write a short book in which I could concentrate on
the romance alone, doing it in larger scope and making it a
detailed and continuous narrative without the distraction
of Herndon's fabrications. *The Courtship of Mr. Lincoln*
presents his wooing as historical evidence shows it. In some
cases account must be taken of conflicting evidence. This
book is not fictionalized; the original manuscript in my possession has full documentation. It is based to a large extent
on letters written at the time, especially letters written by
Miss Todd and Mr. Lincoln themselves. Since the subject
of the courtship has been much fictionalized in plays and
novels, some may be interested in knowing what is based
on historical evidence.

It is a purpose of biography to bring to life individuals
of the past. I have tried to recover the personalities of Abraham Lincoln and Mary Todd, as they were in the days of
young manhood and womanhood. (The narrative is interrupted in chapters eight and nine in order to round out
their full portraits in maturity.) I have attempted to follow
their lives in the years from 1839 to 1842 almost day by
day, as far as the evidence will permit, and to trace in their
letters their psychological changes in this period. In Lincoln's case one of the most interesting and significant experiences of his religious growth was connected with his
courtship. He tells how he struggled out of an agonizing
condition in which he was "the most miserable man living"

to a spiritual faith when, as he said, he was ready to "Stand
still and see the salvation of the Lord."

The book is meant to be somewhat of a period piece.
Unpublished passages from the fascinating love letters of
James C. Conkling and Mercy Levering and the appealing
letters of Matilda Edwards (all close friends of Mary Todd
whose lives became entangled in the events of the courtship) are like magic charms for transporting one back to the
atmosphere of the time. It has been my wish, however im-
perfectly accomplished, that the story may seem as alive as
it has to me in the writing, that the reader may also escape
from the present-day state of things to walk the unpaved
streets of early Springfield, Illinois (taking care not to
mire down at the muddy crossings), to meet there certain
very human and lovable people, and to live with them
through strange and absorbing events which occurred more
than a century ago.

Friends, as always, have been most generous in giving
help. In the larger sense all to whom I expressed acknowledgment in *Mary Lincoln: Biography of a Marriage* deserve
it here also. The years of research which went into the
preparation of that book filled my files with more material
and leads than I could do justice to in that one volume.

I am especially indebted to Anna Cushman Glover for
information about her grandmother, Anna Caesaria Rodney
Cushman, bridesmaid at the Lincoln-Todd wedding.

Professor Richard N. Current, who completed *Last Full
Measure*, Volume IV of *Lincoln the President*, which my
husband, J. G. Randall, left unfinished at his death, has

read the whole manuscript of *The Courtship of Mr. Lincoln* and given helpful comments. Margaret Flint, reference librarian of the Illinois State Historical Library, has read the Bibliographical Note and has been ready to help at all times. For all of this invaluable assistance I am most grateful.

In writing this book I have again had the editorial guidance of Ned Bradford of Little, Brown and Company, a privilege which I deeply appreciate.

Many thanks are due to Lida E. Voight, who stood by in the heat of an Illinois summer to turn untidy handwritten sheets into expertly typed pages of manuscript.

In anything I have written or may write on the Lincoln theme, my greatest debt will always be to my husband, J. G. Randall. Such writing is the outgrowth of those happy years when, as our friends used to say, we were "living with the Lincolns."

R. P. R.

Urbana, Illinois

Contents

List of Illustrations

The Courtship of Mr. Lincoln

CHAPTER 1

Molly Shocks Springfield

ON a certain wet Monday in the winter of 1839–40 a passer-by on the streets of Springfield, Illinois, might have witnessed a scene to make him rub his eyes. Along the miry roadway where the mud was knee-deep in spots came a spattered two-wheeled dray containing a strangely incongruous pair. There was nothing remarkable about the driver — he looked very much as a drayman who did all kinds of hauling ought to look — it was the other figure which would have engaged the bystander's astonished attention.

The dray carried a passenger, a pretty, fashionably dressed young lady. She was becomingly plump, a little under medium height, and had vivid blue eyes, fair skin, and light chestnut hair. She was quite the brightest object in the whole drab scene. Red came quickly to her cheeks and she was doubtless flushed at this time with a feeling of adventure and that special exhilaration which comes to the spirited young when violating their elders' sense of propriety. Her oldest sister, Elizabeth, wife of Ninian W. Edwards, Springfield's top aristocrat, would undoubtedly scold her for making herself conspicuous in this fashion.

The girl's name was Mary Todd; her intimate friends

called her by her nickname Molly. She was on her way to the Edwards home, for she was living there now, and Elizabeth might well say in the exasperated words she was to use on a momentous day then more than two years in the future: "Do not forget that you are a Todd." Elizabeth never forgot she was a Todd and furthermore a leader in Springfield's exclusive "Edwards clique." Mary well knew no one would ever catch Mrs. Ninian W. Edwards riding through the streets of Springfield with a common drayman.

This was how the strange spectacle had come about. Springfield had been having a prolonged rainy spell which made its notorious mud more impossible than ever. Womenkind had been housebound in consequence. In the raw little prairie town just emerging from frontier conditions, sidewalks, if a street had any at all, were apt to be boards loosely laid down, and like as not these had been uprooted by the hogs which had the freedom of the city. Street crossings were so appalling that only hip boots of a future day would have been adequate for negotiating them. But proper Victorian females wore long trailing skirts and would have blushed at the very thought of disclosing that they had ankles or, worse still, "limbs"; the word "legs" would have been too shocking to use. Polite society apparently held firmly to the theory that ladies' feet were pinned on to the bottom of their petticoats.

Mud or no mud, Mary wanted to go downtown. Then and later, when she wanted anything, she wanted it intensely and was apt to do something about getting it. She thought of a plan. She knew where she could get a bundle of shingles; why not take the shingles and drop them one at a time in front of her and step from shingle to shingle to keep out of the mud? She would ask her dear friend Mercy Levering, who was spending the winter at the home of her brother Lawrason Levering, next door to the Edwardses, to join her in this adventure.

The two girls, "both elegantly attired," set out on their expedition. But the plan which had seemed so clever in the making proved to have unexpected difficulties. Shingles were a slender defense against the depth of the mud and by the time they had reached the downtown section, both girls were dreading the journey home. It was a dreary and laborious prospect. At this moment along came a dray used for hauling and Mary had another inspiration; they would get the driver, a little man named Ellis Hart, to haul them home. Mercy was shocked at the idea; her brother would be very much displeased if she did anything so unconventional and forward as that. But Molly saw no reason to drag her skirts through the mire when she could ride. The dray received one passenger and the story leaves Mercy, with her propriety intact, stuck in the mud.

As the vehicle creaked and spattered its way past the nondescript shops and modest homes with their small-town yards and gardens, it passed a well-known gentleman of the town with a pleasant name, Dr. Elias Merryman, who was closely acquainted with Mary and her circle of friends. In his astonishment he called out the obvious question as to what in the world she was doing and received a cheerful and spirited reply. The situation struck his sense of humor and his bent for rhyming. He wrote a gay jingle which has preserved the details of the story.

As I walked out on Monday last
A wet and muddy day
'Twas there I saw a pretty lass
A riding on a dray . . .
Quoth I sweet lass, what do you there
Said she good lack a day
I had no coach to take me home
So I'm riding on a dray.

As it passed, the dray created a sensation:

Up flew windows, out popped heads,
To see this Lady gay
In silken cloak and feathers white
A riding on a dray.

The two big wheels left the little shops behind (some
wearing their names in the style of tavern signs, on a board
swinging in front), continued past diminishing homes,
crossed a little stream, climbed a slope, and stopped in front
of a handsome house set in a grove of trees on a hill. It was
the well-known residence of Mr. and Mrs. Ninian W. Edwards. In the poem at this point, Dr. Merryman's merry
lines take on a teasing note. Molly was undeniably plump
and her friends delighted to poke fun at her about it.

At length arrived at Edwards' gate
Hart backed the usual way
And taking out the iron pin
He rolled her off the dray.

Thus ended an unconventional ride that furnished a topic
of conversation in the town for some time. Some of those
heads that popped out of the windows had strict ideas of
what constituted proper and modest behavior in a young

lady. There was much tut-tutting among Springfield's matrons, especially those, one suspects, who were outside the
pale of the aristocratic clique and hence were not invited
to the Edwards parties. The episode added to Miss Mary
Todd's reputation for being a dashing, spirited, and impulsive young woman.

It had another result. Ellis Hart did not dream he had
passed his otherwise unknown name down to posterity
that day. More than a year later Molly's future husband
would write a famous letter in which he mentioned that
little drayman as the man who once "hauled Molly home."

The girl entered the home in which she had been living
since the fall of 1839. She had come to her sister Elizabeth's
from Lexington, Kentucky, where she had grown up in
the prominent and well-to-do family of her father, Robert S. Todd. For a number of reasons the move to Springfield had seemed desirable. The stately home in Lexington was presided over by a stepmother whose babies had
been arriving with a frequency and regularity soon to be
exemplified by Victoria herself, the little Queen of Eng-
land who was married the winter of this dray ride. Mary
loved babies with passionate maternal instinct, but the
house was overcrowded and the stepmother's hands were
too full. Her own brood made life strenuous enough without the complication of a group of high-spirited stepchil-
dren who furiously resented their father's marrying again.

It was a difficult situation with much to be said on both
sides and it had left its mark on Mary. When her own
mother died, she was a bright, sensitive, impetuous little
girl between six and seven. She and her brothers and sisters

were nervous, headstrong children and one suspects that temper tantrums were no novelty in the household.

Mary's was a disposition that sorely needed a mother's understanding and guidance. Instead there had come the deep-cutting shock of loss to a child's sensitive spirit, then an interval when the disorganized household got along as best it could with the help of her aunt and grandmother. Mary possibly felt under these circumstances that she was an unwanted complication. Then her father married a woman who apparently did not understand Mary's feelings at all. The grandmother, living close by, vigorously and continuously fanned resentment in Mary against this marriage. The result would naturally be that she would resist discipline and training by that stepmother. At all events, she grew up without learning the essential lesson of self-control. She also grew up feeling that a wrong had been done to her, that her childhood in her father's house had been "desolate," and this perhaps was related to the sense of insecurity that always afterward lay beneath her cheerfulness, and to her conviction that she must fight hard to get what she wanted.

It throws light on why she said that Madame Mentelle's boarding school (where she had learned French, dancing, and other social graces) was her real home in her girlhood. It was a finishing school, but, in finishing her young ladies, Madame Mentelle wished it clearly understood that she did not neglect "a truly useful & 'solid' English education in all its branches."

It would be wrong, however, to consider Mary a mere fugitive from a stepmother. There were numerous excellent reasons for going west to make her home with her sister. Springfield had recently become the state capital of Illinois. This meant that the legislature would meet there, bringing many interesting people to town, and among them would undoubtedly be eligible and desirable bachelors. Marriage was about the only career a girl could look forward to, unless she was "strong-minded" or queer, and Mary would have shuddered to have either term applied to her.

Men far outnumbered women in Illinois. At a party in Springfield there were apt to be three or four hundred gentlemen to forty or fifty ladies and like as not half of the feminine contingent was already married or at least engaged. Mary's handsome cousin, John J. Hardin, once suggested with a twinkle that a cargo of girls be brought out in the same manner that a shipload of prospective wives had been taken to colonial Virginia. He thought the entrepreneur could collect at least several head of cattle apiece for his passengers.

Imagination likes to play with this idea, picturing a caravan of stagecoaches moving westward with their heart-fluttering freight, but this undertaking was not necessary: brothers, sisters, and other relatives were attending to the matter. Mary's sister Elizabeth had already invited their sister Frances to Springfield for a long "visit" and with eminent success: Frances was now the wife of a well-to-do physician and druggist of the town, Dr. William Wallace. Elizabeth had the oldest sister's fine sense of looking after the younger ones and Mary was next in age after Frances.

Springfield was full of Todd relatives, all socially prominent and influential, as was usual with the Todds. Outstanding among the fine homes and families in town were those of Dr. John Todd, Mary's uncle, and John Todd Stuart, her cousin, a well-established lawyer. Even if the Todd girls had been lacking in charm, the venture (under such conditions of supply and demand) would probably have been successful, but quite the contrary was true. They were attractive and beautifully qualified socially by birth and rearing. Miss Mary Todd, with dimples and a bright smile, a warm and vivacious personality, and a nimble wit, had all the proper requirements.

She had learned to speak French at Madame Mentelle's. She could recite poetry for hours on end and could write gay verses of her own. Literature was a matter of intense interest to her. But almost everything in her lighthearted young world interested her: plays or pranks, sewing circles or sociables, bonnets or babies. In spite of being mercurial, hers was a sunny temperament and most of the time the sunshine could be counted upon.

She was impulsive, friendly, democratic, affectionate, talkative, and companionable; she was also, like all the Todds, touchy and quick to take offense, apt to fly off the handle and say cutting things which, in the remorse that invariably followed, she regretted with bitter tears. No one would ever drive this girl, but she could be led by her affections, which were warm and deep. The dominance of her affections over all other considerations would in the end set her feet upon a winding path that led to the White House.

CHAPTER 2

The Coterie and "a Mighty Rough Man"

THE threshold Mary stepped over as she entered the Edwards home after her dray ride was one certain to be crossed by all the distinguished visitors who came to town. Ninian Wirt Edwards was the son of Governor Ninian Edwards and his home was the center for the elite of Springfield.

The younger group who flocked there called themselves the "Coterie." It is a word of French origin; one wonders whether Mary suggested it. A gayer or livelier circle or one that included more interesting individuals would be hard to imagine. It seethed with interest in literary and dramatic matters, in politics and all the happenings in a young state capital in a young and growing part of the country. The coterie went through a continual round of exciting events: parties of various kinds, dances, sleigh rides in winter, picnics in summer.

Among the young men of the coterie political ambitions ran high, with plans looking toward that bright nebulous array of thrilling possibilities which is youth's view of the future. But none could know that fate would in time make several of its members Senators and one of them President of the United States. It is well to take a closer look at some of the gentlemen who belong to the dramatis personae of this story.

A young Kentuckian who kept a store was much in evidence. He had a pleasing personality and a handsome Byronic face with a romantic aspect that was very appropriate, as he was apt to fall in love with practically every pretty girl he encountered. It is hardly to be wondered at that when he finally met the girl he was to marry, he was a bit confused about whether his love for her was genuine. The problem was to plunge him into an acute case of melancholia and a famous correspondence. His name was Joshua Speed.

There was a personable young lawyer from the East and a graduate of Princeton, James C. Conkling, who wrote delightfully gossipy letters brimming with humor. He was courting that dear friend of Molly's, Mercy Levering. It may as well be said at once that Mercy's "visit" was going to be successful. James Conkling became her fiancé, although she returned to her home in Baltimore for a while before their marriage, which makes it possible now to read the love letters they wrote each other, letters of wonderful charm and warm personality. Postage at the time for a long distance was twenty-five cents for a single sheet, regardless of size, so the lovers wrote in one direction of the paper, then turned the sheet and wrote across the part already written. It was perhaps a sporting proposition to see how much could be put on one sheet, a challenge and a pleasant feat.

In one of these letters James Conkling gave a playful description of himself. When Mercy told her parents in the East that she had become engaged to this unknown gentleman in Illinois, he wrote: "How much did you flatter me? I suppose you informed them that I was [a] pretty good looking fellow, notwithstanding my sallow complexion and lanthorn jaws — standing about 5 ft 7½ in my boots. . . ."

A handsome figure which climbed the hill toward the Edwards home was that of James Shields, an Irishman in his early thirties. His broad education in the old country had included training in fencing and his mind would turn naturally toward dueling if his truculent Irish pride were offended. He was witty and gallant, but his gallantry verged on the pompous and ridiculous, so that while the girls often laughed with him, they were apt to laugh at him behind his back. They did not take him as seriously as he took himself. Yet he was a man of parts and he would eventually go to the United States Senate. His statue would one day stand in Statuary Hall in the Capitol at Washington and he would be, strangely enough, the only member of the coterie to achieve that distinction.

One gentleman frequently seen in the Edwards parlor was striking enough to stand out in any crowd. There was something arresting in the massive head, the compelling blue eyes deep-set under dark brows, the intellectual forehead, the pugnacious mouth and chin. His shoulders were square, his voice sonorous and vibrant, and the whole effect of his personality was so suggestive of power that it made no difference that his legs were too short for the rest of

him. The nickname of "Little Giant" suited him to perfection. His name was Stephen A. Douglas and some of the
other members of the coterie were beginning to couple
this name with that of Mary Todd. His was a name too
which would be written large in the nation's history.

Another caller formed a contrast to the "Little Giant"
that was almost ludicrous; he was about six feet four, a foot
taller than Douglas. Where Douglas's legs were too short
for his body, this man's legs were disproportionately long.
The head atop the long, lean figure gave no impression of
massiveness, though the dark unruly hair had, as he himself
once said, "a way of getting up as far as possible in the
world." No aggressiveness or pugnacity was in his kind
and rugged face, but the mouth showed quiet strength and
determination. The deep-set gray eyes were often lighted
with an infectious twinkle, but at times they held a look of
loneliness and sadness.

It was said that Abraham Lincoln walked "loosely"; his
movements were slow and some called them awkward, yet
others thought he managed his long bones with a natural
simplicity and economy of motion. His voice was high-
pitched and had a singular quality that one had to get used
to, but it carried well when he was speaking to a crowd.
His words among the well-educated members of the coterie
had at times a backwoods twang or flavor that set him
apart. Sometimes the homely, sensitive face showed a wistfulness for approval, for a sense of belonging.

He knew the members of the coterie had the advantage
of him in background and training. Their parents had not
been so lowly and ignorant as his. They had mostly gone to

academies and colleges, while his short periods of attendance at primitive backwoods schools, added up, did not exceed a year. And he had had to educate himself under most adverse circumstances.

He had been born in a log cabin in Kentucky in 1809 and had had a few weeks at a tiny school in that state before his family moved to Indiana when he was seven. From then until he was twenty-one he lived the bone-bare existence of a pioneer family in the Indiana wilderness. It included some months of rudimentary schooling, but he was surrounded by people who used "whar" for where, "hearn" for heard, "cheer" for chair, "kase" for because, and many other expressions that would stick out like sore thumbs in a cultured group. But there was something in the tall and ungainly youth that made him reach out for knowledge and "book-larning," as those around him might have called it.

After his family moved to Illinois and he left his father's log cabin to make his own way, he went to a little Illinois village consisting of one long street on a bluff over the Sangamon River, New Salem. There he was associated with people who had more education than those he had known up to that time, which meant much in giving him standards in the self-education he was struggling to achieve. The six years in New Salem were years of prodigious growth. He became village postmaster, he learned surveying, studied grammar, and read law. In several years, the people, liking his qualities, sent him to the state legislature at Vandalia. The next move was to Springfield in April 1837, when he was twenty-eight. So much for the elements that had gone into the building-up of this unusual personality which had recently become a member of the coterie.

He was an artist at telling droll stories and his characteristic, resounding laugh was like a tonic. There was also a magical change when a smile lighted up the sober features. People liked and trusted this man and enjoyed being with him. It probably did not occur to many of the lighthearted coterie, who were more apt to talk of his oddities, that he had a tremendous magnetism. Many elements entered into that magnetism: kindliness and interest in people, compassionate understanding, humor and whimsicality, scrupulous honesty, and a deep reserve of intellectual power.

Again peeping into the private correspondence of Mr. Conkling with his betrothed, one finds a description of this Lincoln as he appeared to the more self-assured members of the coterie: "He used to remind me sometimes of the pictures I formerly saw of old Father Jupiter, bending down from the clouds, to see what was going on below. And as an agreeable smile of satisfaction graced the countenance of the old heathen god, as he perceived the incense rising up — so the face of L. was occasionally distorted into a grin as he succeeded in eliciting applause from some of the fair votaries by whom he was surrounded."

The Edwards circle was an excellent one in which to hear who was who and why, and Molly undoubtedly knew several important items about this Mr. Lincoln before she met him. She may have heard her brother-in-law Ninian mention that he had been a fellow member in the state legislature at Vandalia; in fact, Mr. Edwards and Mr. Lincoln had belonged to the special tall group from Sangamon

County which had been dubbed the "Long Nine." Their combined heights exceeded fifty-four feet and no one was taller than Lincoln.

Mr. Edwards had been friendly to the countrified young lawyer in his early days in Springfield, though he considered Mr. Lincoln at that time "a mighty Rough man." Lincoln had frequently been among those who spent Sunday at the hospitable Edwards home. Mrs. Edwards remembered later that he and Joshua Speed came out together and "seemed to enjoy themselves in their conversation beneath the dense shade of our forest trees." Trees are appreciated in a prairie town and it was undoubtedly pleasant on sunny days to leave the more built-up, unshaded section around the square and walk out to the wooded hill, especially as the unsanitary village (including the privies which adorned the back yards), was apt on hot days to be a bit smelly.

Much more important than Mr. Lincoln's initial friendship with Ninian was the fact that Molly's cousin, John Todd Stuart, had taken him as his junior law partner when he came to Springfield. It is doubtful if anyone had described to her that humble arrival, Mr. Lincoln riding into the center of town on a borrowed horse with all his earthly possessions in two bags slung over the saddle, and stopping in front of Joshua Speed's store on the west side of the square. It had happened more than two years before she came to live with the Edwardses.

This law partnership meant a great deal, for "Cousin John" occupied a position in which he could choose a partner who offered excellent qualifications. Mr. Lincoln must have distinct abilities. The Stuart & Lincoln law office had an upstairs location in Hoffman's Row on Fifth Street just north of the public square which was the heart of Springfield. In its center stood the new capitol, or state house, which was still in the process of being built, as the piles of stone and building litter scattered around it indicated. Mr. Lincoln could feel a personal sense of pride in watching the construction of that building; the tap of the hammers was doubtless a pleasant sound to him. At Vandalia he had worked hard to have the capital removed to Springfield. This meant so much to the straggling town that there had been wild rejoicing when the news arrived, ending in a huge bonfire around the whipping post on the east side of the square. One pictures the loyal citizens prancing around it like college boys after a football victory.

Somehow the little town had a personality which reminds one of a growing youth, undeveloped and unpredictable as yet, but full of enthusiasm, ambition, vitality, and curiosity. In the people who walked or loitered around the square was a great eagerness to know more, from the least detail of gossip to wonderful new "Discoveries, Inventions, and Improvements," to borrow the title of a notable lecture Mr. Lincoln would one day deliver in the town. It was an age which had not lost its sense of wonder.

The square was the center of Mr. Lincoln's life as well as the center of town. He was living in the big bedroom over Speed's store on the west side of it, 103 South Fifth Street. When he had come to town, Joshua had taken him in as a roommate after finding Lincoln had no money for lodgings. (And what a congenial and affectionate friendship theirs had turned out to be!) When the young lawyer started to his office in the morning, he had only to turn to the left, cross Washington Street, and climb the stairs at 109 North Fifth Street to enter the Stuart & Lincoln law office. As a matter of personal enjoyment he might have preferred to turn right on Washington, walk along the north boundary of the square, and cross the street to the office of the *Sangamo Journal* on North Sixth. This was the newspaper of Mr. Lincoln's own party, the Whig, and fiercely partisan, as papers and people in Springfield were apt to be.

The furniture of the office was doubtless similar to that of a later one on Sixth Street: "a large wood stove, which stood in a box of sand occupying about 3 x 5 feet," an "editorial table" (probably of the kitchen variety), and some common wooden chairs. But when this bare interior was lighted on winter days by the glow of the stove and the chairs in a circle around it were occupied by Springfield's most resourceful Whigs exchanging lively ideas, it became for Mr. Lincoln a forum after his own heart. A newspaper office always has fascination for the politically ambitious and the editor of the *Journal*, Simeon Francis, was one of Lincoln's best friends, so he spent a great deal of time there. What a glowing editorial Simeon had written after Lincoln and the other members of the Long Nine had been victorious in transferring the capital to Springfield! That editorial of praise was a sort of introduction for Mr. Lincoln when he came to town. The block where the *Journal* had its office was to be an important one for him in more ways than one; at the end of it was the home of Mr. and Mrs. Francis, which is to be the setting for memorable scenes in this story.

In after years, according to her sister Emilie, Mary delighted to tell of her first meeting with Mr. Lincoln. "He met me at a party," she would say, "and at last came awkwardly forward and said: 'Miss Todd, I want to dance with you in the worst way.'" At this point in her telling, no doubt with her damaged slippers in mind, she would add with a little bubble of laughter, "And he surely did."

One can well imagine the candle-lighted scene: the society girls of more than a century ago in their billowing wide-skirted frocks (as nearly like the prints in *Godey's Lady's Book* as possible) and the stiff young gallants with their sideburns, stocks, slim trousers, and long-tailed coats. To Molly dainty clothes of the latest style were very important. One can be sure that her white shoulders, rounded little figure, and bright face were set off to advantage and well calculated to be followed by the eyes of the tall young lawyer who was Cousin John's junior partner.

Since Miss Todd and Mr. Lincoln moved in the same gregarious circle, other meetings followed as a matter of course. Each possibly had from the first a special awareness of the other and an attentive ear for any chance remark concerning the new acquaintance. Mary's friendly curiosity was much too lively and feminine for her not to find out about this Mr. Lincoln.

It probably did not take her long to discover that he was the devoted friend of Joshua Speed and that he was sharing Joshua's rooms over the store. A couple of clerks also slept in the big room and in the winter evenings the young men often gathered with other friends around the potbellied stove in the store below to argue, tell robust stories, and discuss men, politics, philosophy, and the universe in general. It was a roughhewn man's environment of which Molly knew little; its conversations were far removed from her chattered feminine confidences with other girls in the Edwards home. The division between man's world and woman's world was much more sharply defined in the eighteen-hundreds than it is today.

It is doubtful whether she knew that Joshua had taken Mr. Lincoln in and given him free lodging because he was so poor and in debt to boot. A loyal friend and thorough Kentucky gentleman like Joshua was not apt to mention such a subject.

This Mr. Lincoln had a way of giving and inspiring genuine friendships. William Butler, an older friend and also a Kentuckian, helped him out by giving him free board. When he was ready to eat, he had only to walk a few blocks northwest of the square to the Butler home, where the kindly Mrs. Butler would attend to the matter. He went when he was ready, which was often late, for Mr. Lincoln was never to be regimented into keeping regular meal hours. But the Butlers found that even so "his company was worth his keep." The Butler offspring loved him and would run to meet him when he came. He would lift one of the youngsters high in the air, toss him over his shoulder, and laugh and romp with all the children.

Early in that year when Mary came to Springfield a sharp incident had shown William Butler what a good man Mr. Lincoln was to have around when one's hotheadedness got out of hand. William, hearing of certain political moves in which Lincoln and their mutual friend Edward D. Baker had had a part, jumped to the conclusion that he had been badly treated by them and, without waiting to get all the facts, went off half cocked and wrote each of them a fiery letter. (Both men were out of town at Vandalia.) Lincoln kept his temper when he received his and answered frankly but without heat: "You were in an ill-humor when you wrote that letter, and, no doubt, intended that I should be thrown into one also; which, however, I respectfully decline being done." He then carefully explained all the facts, showing Butler that no wrong had been done to him, and ended the letter "Your friend in spite of your ill-nature Lincoln."

But Mr. Baker did not take the letter he received with so much detachment. He promptly fired back at Butler a hot answer, saying among other things: "If you believe the charges you make to be true, I say most flatly you are a fool." A serious altercation was in the making.

Lincoln gave sincere affection to both men. One gets a close-up view of certain qualities of his in learning how he went about patching up the difficulty between what he called "two of my most particular friends." He wrote Butler calmly and reasonably: "There is no necessity for any bad feeling between Baker & yourself. Your first letter to him was written while you were in a state of high excitement, and therefore ought not to have been construed as an emination of deliberate malice. Unfortunately however it reached Baker while he was writhing under a severe tooth-ache. . . ." Lincoln pointed out that Baker's tooth-ache letter should not be taken too seriously either, such an ailment tending to warp patience and judgment, and continued: "It is always magnanamous to recant whatever we may have said in passion; and when you and Baker shall have done this, I am sure there will no difficulty be left between you." (One has here examples of how Mr. Lincoln would occasionally slip up on the spelling of a word, a fact not to be wondered at when it is remembered that he was at this time still very much in the process of educating himself.)

It was a skillful settling of a quarrel that conceivably could have developed into a duel. Lincoln was a reliable, agreeable, and helpful fellow to have around, a good-neighbor sort of person.

Molly could sense that Mr. Lincoln was older than she was. As a matter of fact, he had had his thirtieth birthday the February before he met her and she was twenty-one in December 1839, so the difference in ages was nearly ten years. He may have seemed even older, for hardship had put lines and hollows in his lean face.

He seems to have been drawn toward girls much younger than himself. An attractive member of the coterie was Anna C. Rodney, a pretty, brown-eyed girl who was even younger than Molly. She was mentioned in both a letter of Miss Todd's and one of Mr. Conkling's, but they did not happen to tell that Mr. Lincoln, according to the tradition which has come down in Anna's family, sometimes called on her, inquiring for her in his quaint fashion: "Is Miss Rodney handy?" Anna, who was from the East, was another of those marriageable girls who had come to Springfield to "visit" an older sister.

Miss Todd probably read some articles Mr. Lincoln was

writing for the local papers that fall. One dealt with a matter of state banks on which Democrats and Whigs were not in agreement. Mary could not know that before long a dispute involving the two political parties and state banks was destined to put Mr. Lincoln in actual physical danger and result in a fearful experience for both of them, one for which each took a measure of blame.

Mary knew that Mr. Lincoln, thank heaven, was as ardent a Whig as she was, and worked at it. In fact he was a rather busy man in his slow, unhurried way. That was a soothing quality of his: never to be hurried, but always to be deliberate in thinking things out before acting. She tended to rush into speech and action without due consideration. Still, slowness can sometimes be exasperating to one of her impatient temperament. He in turn may have found her quick decisiveness very attractive compared with his slow groping toward decisions.

That fall of 1839 Mr. Lincoln had the entire responsibility of the Stuart & Lincoln law office after Cousin John left for Washington to take a seat in Congress. When he departed early in November, the junior partner wrote a whimsical memorandum in the firm's fee book: "Commencement of Lincoln's Administration." (There was nothing in the humble fortunes of this self-doubting man to suggest that one day the term "Lincoln's Administration" would assume a nationwide significance.)

After the legislature met early in December – their first meeting in Springfield – it is easy to follow Mr. Lincoln's activities in that body. People talked a bit about a speech he made the day after Christmas; it was so powerful and logical that one newspaper called it "a speech which no man can answer. . . ." Molly read political articles in the papers, though she had a half-guilty feeling in doing it, and she probably knew of this speech and perhaps also of a remarkable lecture he had given before she came to live with her sister. The gentlemen of Springfield took their intellectual betterment very seriously. Such improvement was the aim of the organization known as the Young Men's Lyceum, which Lincoln had addressed on the subject "The Perpetuation of Our Political Institutions." He might be weak on spelling, but it was a speech which showed deep thinking and a power of putting complex matters into language that was wonderfully effective in its clarity and simplicity. It also had a certain poetic quality, a verve which was apparent in its opening words: "In the great journal of things happening under the sun, we, the American People, find our account running, under date of the nineteenth century of the Christian era."

Mary could recognize that this man, though he was sometimes ill at ease in society, was very much at home in working out political problems and presenting them aptly. Brains and good literary expression always delighted her. After she had visited Mrs. Edwards in the summer of 1837, she returned to Lexington and continued her studies under the guidance of dear Dr. Ward, who taught both boys and girls in Ward's Academy. It was not enough that she had been "finished" at Madame Mentelle's school; she wanted to do what might be called postgraduate work. Dr. John Ward, Episcopal minister and a cultured, learned gentleman who ahead of his time believed in coeducation, could lead an eager student far in the literary kingdom of the eighteen-thirties.

It is likely that Mary's older sisters, centered in the domestic duties which were supposed to encompass woman's sphere, sniffed a bit at her excursions into literary matters and called her a "bluestocking" or, as Mary herself used the term, "a regular blue." Any settled Victorian matron knew a woman's interests should be purely domestic and that she should leave all kinds of intellectual activities to her husband, after she had accomplished another paramount feminine duty by acquiring one.

If Mary came quickly to an appreciation of Mr. Lincoln's intellectual power, her two sisters living in Springfield were unimpressed. Mrs. Edwards was quick to detect the gaps in his education and as far as she was concerned, he was uninteresting. Mary's sister Frances, now successfully married to Dr. Wallace, took an equally dim view of Cousin John's junior partner. When she had had the role of the visiting sister at the Edwards home before Mary came, Lincoln had taken her out on one or two occasions, but assuredly no intangible forces of attraction went into operation between the two. Quite the contrary. Frances's verdict, given years later, was that ". . . he was not much for society. He would go where they took him, but he was never very much for company." This certainly does not sound as if she enjoyed going out with him and one doubts whether Mr. Lincoln had a good time either. An interesting comparison between Frances and Mary Todd as young girls was given by their cousin Elizabeth Humphreys; she liked Frances but thought she "was taciturn and seemed cold & reserved," while Mary "was bright and talkative & warm hearted."

The chilly appraisals of her sisters did not influence Mary in her interest in her new friend. Meanwhile what was he discovering about her?

It was no trouble at all for Mr. Lincoln to find out about that attractive little Miss Todd. She was much in evidence and took a lively part in all the activities of Springfield's top social circle. He heard about the dray ride, probably with warm liking for the girl's spunk and defiance of convention, not to mention her natural democracy in riding with a drayman. It is possible he even saw the incident. Anyhow, Dr. Merryman's verses about it circulated in the coterie and Mr. Lincoln must have read them, doubtless with a twinkle that broke into a laugh at the line "He rolled her off the dray." Some day he would enjoy teasing Mary himself.

At parties he could see her as Mr. Conkling once described her to his fiancée: "She is the very creature of excitement you know and never enjoys herself more than when in society and surrounded by a company of merry friends." She usually was so "surrounded," as a gay and entertaining girl who loves people is likely to be.

CHAPTER 3

"I . . . Made a Fool of Myself"

THERE was no doubt that Miss Todd was good company. But Mr. Lincoln found that her conversation had learning and substance as well as sparkle. In this she may have reminded him of the young woman he had been courting back in New Salem the year before he came to Springfield to live. Her name was Mary too — Mary Owens. That courtship was a closed incident by the time he met Miss Todd, but it was still fresh and uncomfortable in his memory.

Miss Owens also had had an excellent education and social background and was an entertaining and intelligent conversationalist. And, like Miss Todd, she had a certain sprightliness (not to say sauciness) of retort, a sort of provocative coquetry that was very attractive. Lincoln liked the light verbal fencing of repartee and was good at it himself in a pleasing and whimsical way. It was an era when the snappy comeback was well thought of.

His wooing of Miss Owens, however, had been a tepid affair, one that left him feeling as if he should make a wry face at himself. That is practically what he did when, after it was all over, he wrote a full account of it to a good friend, Mrs. Orville H. Browning, whom he had come to know well when he was at Vandalia. Her husband had been his friend and fellow Whig in the legislature there. Mrs. Browning was a woman of kindliness, humor, and considerable force of mind. (One is beginning to note that Mr. Lincoln preferred intelligent women.) She was understanding, or he never would have written her this letter which ended on the note that he had "made a fool" of himself. He may have selected April Fool's Day (April 1, 1838) as the date on which to write it with an eye to its appropriateness.

As his pen unfolded the comedy to Mrs. Browning, one can picture him writing with alternate twinkle and grimace. He had been greatly pleased with Miss Owens when he had first met her back in 1833 at New Salem, where she was visiting her sister Mrs. Bennett Abell. Lincoln was fond of Mrs. Abell and sometimes stayed at the Abell home; those had been good friends and neighbors in and around New Salem, though they did not live in the style of some of the people of Springfield.

Three years later, in the fall of 1836, Mrs. Abell told him she was going back to her old home in Kentucky for a visit and added as a gay challenge that she would bring back an attractive sister of hers if he would promise to marry her; or, as Lincoln himself expressed it, "upon condition that I would engage to become her brother-in-law with all convenient dispach." Of course, as a gallant gentleman he had to meet the challenge and agree to the proposition, but there was more to it than this: he remembered well how very desirable he had considered Miss Owens when she had visited her sister before.

She had perhaps the best educated feminine mind he had

encountered up to that time. Furthermore, her mind could do some thinking of its own. That she rebelled against the narrow bounds set down for female conduct is evident in a letter she wrote from Kentucky in 1835 to Thomas J. Nance, an old friend who had gone to Illinois. She boldly broke the rule that a lady must not write to a gentleman unless he first has written to her. "You are well aware Thomas," she said, "that in writing you this letter, I am transgressing the circumscribed limits, laid down by tyrranical custom, for our sex." She defended herself vigorously: "Wherein consists the impropriety of my corresponding with an absent Friend, and admiting at the same time, that Friend to be a Gentleman? We are beings formed for social intercourse, and I hold it admissable for us, to draw pleasure from what ever source we can, provided, it be an innocent one." She did not care if narrowminded individuals did criticize her: ". . . if I am condemned by the cold, unfeeling and fastidious of either Sex, I care not, for I trust, my Heart, has learned to rise superior to those groveling feelings, dictated by bosoms, that are callous to every refined emotion." She had learned that Thomas was coming to Kentucky and proper maidenly reserve went so far out of bounds as to allow her to write him she was "much pleased" about his coming and to make this leading statement: ". . . you have many Friends here, whose Hearts beat high, at the thought of seeing you again, for my own part, I frankly acknowledge, that to me, it would be a treat of no every day occurence, to see Thomas, and talk about days of Auld lang Sine."

The unconventional and liberal-minded Mr. Lincoln

could have stimulating conversation with such an independent thinker. They could discuss politics and books and she could satisfy in a way his hunger for intellectual companionship. He thought there was much to be said for Mrs. Abell's proposition. "I was most confoundedly well pleased with the project," he wrote. "I had seen the said sister some three years before, thought her inteligent and agreeable, and saw no good objection to plodding life through hand in hand with her."

The conversation with Mrs. Abell had been half in fun, of course, a matter of banter between them. Lincoln was twenty-seven at this time and had a natural interest in girls and the thought of getting married, but he also had a marriage shyness that is sometimes encountered in sensitive young men. Then, too, ever since he had left his father's backwoods cabin five years before, he had been engaged in that difficult task sometimes described as "pulling himself up by his bootstraps" and so far it may have seemed to him that there had been more pulling than elevation. He was having a hard enough time taking care of himself without assuming any additional responsibility in the shape of a wife and possible family.

He was therefore considerably startled when word came to his ears that Mrs. Abell had returned from Kentucky and had brought her sister Mary with her. This seemed too much like pinning him down. It was one thing to jest with Mrs. Abell about marrying her sister and another to have that sister here in the flesh.

"Flesh" is just the word! When he came face to face with Miss Owens, he discovered she had gotten fat! Three years of good Kentucky fare in her well-to-do home in that state had added poundage that was not conducive to romance, and besides, she had lost some teeth. It made her look much older and, as a matter of fact, she was about a year older than he was. A "weather-beaten appearance in general," to use his own words, put "a kind of notion" in his head "that *nothing* could have commenced at the size of infancy, and reached her present bulk in less than thirtyfive or forty years. . . ."

He probably would not have noted these changes so critically if it had not been for that commitment to her sister which now hung heavily on his conscience. Of course, Miss Owens still had her fine mind and was as intelligent and entertaining to talk with as ever. And she would have been quite handsome if she had not put on so much weight. No one could deny that she had a very fine face. "I also tried to convince myself, that the mind was much more to be valued than the person," wrote Lincoln describing his disturbed cogitations.

His extreme conscientiousness was always to cause him mental anguish. If Miss Owens had already reached an age when she was considered an old maid and he himself failed to find her physically attractive, perhaps no other man would want her either and he was her last chance. A far-flung conjecture arises here. If her unmaidenly intimation to Thomas Nance that her heart "beat high" at the thought of seeing him again had indicated romantic leanings on the part of Miss Owens toward that gentleman, it is possible she had had a disappointment when he married another lady in September of that very autumn when Mrs. Abell made her proposition to Mr. Lincoln. It is even possible New Salem gossip had suggested such a thing to him. Was the married sister sympathetically hoping Mr. Lincoln would console Mary Owens? At all events, he felt he had committed himself to marry her. "Through life I have been in no bondage, either real or immaginary from the thraldom of which I so much desired to be free." He spent his time, he said, in planning "how I might procrastinate the evil day for a time, which I really dreaded as much — perhaps more, than an irishman does the halter." (Part of this feeling was a wariness about marriage itself.)

So the courtship which was missing on a number of cylinders limped along. Miss Owens was not finding Mr. Lincoln entirely satisfactory either. By great good fortune one has her account of the affair as well as his. Lincoln had been mistaken in thinking it her destiny to become an old maid: later another gentleman was found who saw no objection to plodding through life hand in hand with the lady. She had long been a wife and mother when she described her feeling about Mr. Lincoln. Posterity encounters no reticence about this courtship; it has very frank statements from both of the parties concerned, and nowhere does one intrude upon a deep or tender sentiment.

Miss Owens felt that Lincoln "was deficient in those little links which make up the great chain of womans happiness." She apparently missed in him social niceties and gallantries that had been no part of his background or training up to that time.

There was one occasion when a number of New Salem's younger set were riding on horseback from the little village to a party at "Uncle Billy Greens." Mr. Lincoln was Miss Owens's escort. They came to "a very bad branch to cross" and all the other gentlemen solicitously saw to it that their ladies made the crossing in safety, but Lincoln rode on ahead without looking back and left Miss Owens to shift for herself. She was piqued and, riding up beside him, said tartly: ". . . you are a nice fellow; I suppose you did not care whether my neck was broken or not." Lincoln laughed and defended himself with a rather forced compliment, saying he knew she was "plenty smart" enough to take care of herself.

But he was sensitive and self-doubting and that sort of criticism would only add to his marriage shyness. It was not the only time she made a critical remark. There was another occasion when they were in a little group which was climbing the hill to Mrs. Abell's home. One of the matrons was carrying her baby, a large and heavy child, and Miss Owens thought that Lincoln should have helped her. Looking to the future in a realistic way, she decided he would not make a thoughtful husband and she bluntly told him so. The detached reasoning and plain speaking that characterized this romance on both sides is very impressive.

And yet Miss Owens did comprehend Mr. Lincoln's sensitive kindness of heart. She remembered how he told her once of an incident when this quality of his worked to his undoing. He had been crossing the prairie one day, he said, "fixed up" rather better than usual, when he saw a pig mired down in the mud and unable to free itself. He knew he would ruin his appearance if he undertook the messy task of rendering aid, so he steeled himself to pass on by.

But he was drawn irresistibly to look back and he could not
endure the hopeless look in the animal's eyes. Back he went,
got down in the mud, and worked the prisoner free, ruin-
ing his clothes in the process but leaving his tender conscience unhaunted.

Miss Owens admitted he was sensitive almost to a fault.
She conceded his good points and he conceded hers. They
saw eye to eye in politics, which was an important factor
with Mr. Lincoln. The trouble plainly was that while there
were mutual interest and a degree of congeniality between
them, neither could succeed in falling in love with the
other. But there was his commitment to Mrs. Abell, and no
other feminine interest was in sight, so the wooing progressed in an uninspired fashion.

While he was attending the meeting of the state legislature at Vandalia in December 1836, he wrote Miss Owens
a dispirited letter. He had been sick, he said, and there was
nothing to write about anyway and furthermore he had
not received the expected letter from her. He had gone to
the post office a number of times and had been mortified at
finding nothing. "You see I am mad about that *old letter*
yet," he wrote. "I dont like verry well to risk you again.
I'll try you once more any how." Here is the first glimpse
of this man's tendency to have the "blues" (or "hypo," as
he usually called it), especially when his vitality was low
after an illness. For all his long brawn, he did have occasional illnesses, his skin was sallow and he was thin. Perhaps
the unbalanced diet with the exposure and hardship of his
growing years had contributed to this.

His letter went on to give Miss Owens in halfhearted

fashion news of what was going on in the legislature. He mentioned his interest in getting the capital transferred to Springfield. His sentiments toward Vandalia as the meeting place were apparent; various things, he wrote, "have gotten my spirits so low, that I feel that I would rather be any place in the world than here. I really can not endure the thought of staying here ten weeks." Would she write back as soon as she got this letter and say something to cheer him up? He ended by admitting his letter was so dry and stupid "that I am ashamed to send it," and he signed himself non-committally "Your friend Lincoln." It can hardly be called a loverlike epistle.

By the spring of 1837 it had been decided that the capital would be removed to Springfield and Lincoln went to live in that town. Apparently by this time the courtship had progressed somewhat and he had broached the question of marriage to Miss Owens without getting any definite answer. From Springfield he wrote "Friend Mary" two notable letters which present a veritable lawyer's brief of reasons why she had better not marry him! He explained at length how drab the prospect would be for her if she did.

He was so poor and could offer a wife so little. The stylishness of Springfield made him realize this acutely: "I am often thinking about what we said of your coming to live at Springfield. I am afraid you would not be satisfied. There is a great deal of flourishing about in carriages here, which it would be your doom to see without shareing in it. You would have to be poor without the means of hiding your poverty. Do you believe you could bear that patiently?"

If she decided to take the risk, however, he would do his

best to make her happy. He would be very unhappy himself if he failed in this, but "I much wish you would think seriously before you decide. . . . My opinion is that you had better not do it. You have not been accustomed to hardship, and it may be more severe than you now immagine."

He hoped she would write him a "good long letter." He needed it for "company" in this "busy wilderness." In all his letters to Miss Owens there is great loneliness between the lines.

A little over three months later he wrote her again. In the meantime he had seen her, but apparently the situation between them remained as unsettled as ever. In fact, the interview had been so unsatisfactory that he wrote her later "on the same day on which we parted," trying to clarify matters. She must know that he could not see her or think of her "with entire indifference." (One can imagine Miss Owens's reaction to that anemic compliment.) "I want in all cases to do right," he wrote, "and most particularly so, in all cases with women. I want, at this particular time, more than anything else, to do right with you, and if I *knew* it would be doing right, as I rather suspect it would, to let you alone, I would do it."

She was free to drop the whole matter and leave his letter unanswered, if that was what suited her best and would make her happiest; their further friendship depended upon her, but, "Do not understand by this, that I wish to cut your acquaintance." His greatest wish was to consider her happiness, and "to make myself understood, is the only object of this letter."

If their friendship was to continue, he wanted to know

her exact feelings. "If it suits you best to not answer this — farewell — a long life and a merry one attend you. But if you conclude to write back, speak as plainly as I do." Again he signed himself "Your friend Lincoln."

These are the letters of an upright, honorable man, one with a torturing conscience, lonely, and groping to find an adjusted life, but they are not the letters of a man in love. There was nothing in their sober reasoning calculated to make the prospect of her becoming Mrs. Lincoln romantic, or even cheerful.

By the fall of 1837 Lincoln felt he could stand the uncertainty no longer. To resume his own account of the courtship to Mrs. Browning: "After I had delayed the matter as long as I thought I could in honor do . . . I concluded I might as well bring it to a consumation without further delay; and so I mustered my resolution, and made the proposal to her direct; but, shocking to relate, she answered, No."

He found this hard to believe and at first thought she answered thus "through an affectation of modesty [such being considered delicate and ladylike behavior at the time], but on my renewal of the charge, I found she repeled it with greater firmness than before. . . . I finally was forced to give it up, at which I verry unexpectedly found myself mortified almost beyond endurance." He was especially humiliated that, while absorbed in analyzing his own feelings and intentions, he had been so "stupid" about understanding hers: "and also, that she whom I had taught myself to believe no body else would have, had actually rejected me with all my fancied greatness. . . ."

The whole episode was hard for him to take. As the lady became unattainable (and less of a menace to his bachelor-hood) she became more attractive in his eyes: ". . . and to cap the whole, I then, for the first time, began to suspect that I was really a little in love with her. But let it all go. I'll try and out live it. Others have been made fools of by the girls; but this can never be with truth said of me. I most emphatically, in this instance, made a fool of myself. I have now come to the conclusion never again to think of marrying; and for this reason; I can never be satisfied with any one who would be block-head enough to have me."

So runs Lincoln's own account of this dispassionate woo-ing. He wrote it less than a year after the affair terminated, but he was all over it (except for a sore place in his pride) and ready to make it an amusing narrative in a letter to a friend written on the first of April. The attachment be-tween himself and Miss Owens was simply not the genuine falling in love that leads to marriage; it resembled it as lit-tle as cold water resembles wine.

These letters reveal Mr. Lincoln's thoughts toward tak-ing a wife; they are important to this story. The period of his courtship of Molly Todd was one of growth for him and never did any man suffer more "growing pains."

CHAPTER 4

"This Thing of Living in Springfield"

LINCOLN'S cautious letters to Miss Owens make one smile, but they are also pathetic. They reveal between the lines his loneliness, his reaching out for intelligent companionship, his man's need for a woman's interest and sympathy, his longing for love and for the giving of love. To one who had been knocking about in such homeless fashion, there was perhaps the unconscious wish for a home.

It is possible that the mental congeniality with Miss Owens had served to whet his desire for feminine companionship, that she awakened a longing that she did not satisfy. He found her lacking in sympathetic understanding and in physical appeal.

How different it was with little Miss Todd, with her pretty figure, her vivid, animated face, her quick little gestures of dainty hands! She had the excitability, the enthusiasms, and the joyousness of a child. Miss Owens had been older than Lincoln and everything about her heavy figure had suggested maturity to him; Miss Todd, nearly ten years younger, aroused the paternal instinct that was always so strong an element in his make-up.

He was about a foot taller than Molly; the head with bright chestnut hair hardly came to his shoulder. When she stood beside him, he could look down on that bright head and see the sweep of long lashes against the pink curve of her cheek. She was responsive; his playfulness and whimsicality would bring a quick answering smile and the smile in turn would bring a dimple. Like Miss Owens, Miss Todd had a keenly intelligent, well-furnished, and scintillating mind. But with her he did not have to make a reasoned effort to convince himself "that the mind was much more to be valued than the person"; the "person" had all the qualifications too.

Miss Owens had been self-sufficient; she was "plenty smart" enough to take care of herself. One doubts that she was excitable. Miss Todd, with her impulsiveness and her quick tongue that was apt to get her into trouble, undoubtedly needed a slow, balanced, deliberate person like himself to look after her. This dependence makes a paternal man feel necessary and important, where feminine self-sufficiency can make him feel inadequate. For it is one of nature's tricks on young people at the mating age that a man finds a girl's childishness charming and a boost to his masculine sense of protectiveness, when the same quality in a wife of some years' standing may be a problem and an exasperation.

Both of these girls who had caught the attention of young Mr. Lincoln had the appeal of wearing attractive clothes. Miss Todd's daintiness and furbelows were part of her charm for him. In that future unknown married life that destiny held in store for him, he was to notice when his wife wore a new dress and was to admire her when she was arrayed for a party in hoopskirt splendor. Up to the time of his going to live in Springfield, most of the girls he had known had been living in log cabins, cooking over open fireplaces with water carried laboriously from springs. Daintiness, even cleanliness, under such conditions was difficult, and Lincoln's awareness of the contrast between these rural maidens and the style-conscious belles of Springfield was apparent in what he once exclaimed as he entered a ballroom: "Oh — boys, how clean those girls look."

It is hard to picture young Abraham Lincoln in a candle-lit ballroom, to imagine that lanky figure, whose long legs seem more suited to steady striding across the prairie, engaged in the dances of the eighteen-hundreds. It is easy to accept the statement that he was "rather clumsy at dancing." Yet there is concrete proof of his interest in dances by the end of 1839. There exists today a quaintly formal invitation to a "Cotillion Party" given in December at the American House, Springfield's most pretentious hotel which stood on the southeast corner of the square. This dance was being arranged by sixteen "Managers" who are listed on the invitation itself. The name of "A. Lincoln" appears in this list as well as those of other friends already introduced: Stephen A. Douglas, the "Little Giant," James Shields, the blarney-tongued and truculent Irishman, and Joshua Speed, the frequent lover. This invitation makes it plain that by the end of 1839, over two years after he came to Springfield, Lincoln was established in the social whirl of the coterie and was stepping out in society.

He had come so far that he had even, shortly before the cotillion, joined several other enterprising men in sending out an SOS for more girls! With the demand so far exceeding the supply, the lonely gentlemen of Springfield had to resort to desperate measures. Lincoln was a ringleader in the writing of a whimsical appeal to Mrs. Browning, who had been his confidante concerning the affair with Miss Owens. This joint letter "respectfully" informed Mrs. Browning that the undersigned were in great need of her society in Springfield "and therefore humbly pray that your *Honoress* will repair, forthwith to the Seat of Government, bringing in your train all ladies in general, who may be at your command; and all Mr. Browning's sisters in particular." The "faithful & dutiful Petitioners" made extravagant promises: if her "Honoress" would grant their request, they would render due attention and faithful obedience to all her orders, whatever they might be. The letter is about half in Lincoln's hand (and indubitably in his playful manner) and is signed by him. The remainder of the letter seems to be in the handwriting of John J. Hardin, Mary's cousin, who also signed it, as did E. B. Webb. (How that Don Juan of Springfield, Joshua Speed, failed to be in on a project like this remains a mystery.) Edwin B. Webb was a widower and his eyes, like Mr. Lincoln's, were beginning to follow the pleasing little figure of Miss Todd.

This letter to Mrs. Browning was enclosed with another in the same vein written by John J. Hardin; the two epistles together take one directly into the intimate, bantering, funmaking atmosphere of the younger set. One can picture the grins with which these friends put their heads together to concoct their urgent appeal. Mr. Hardin's letter promised Mrs. Browning even greater privileges: "In consideration of our distressed situation Mr Butler [at whose home Lincoln boarded] has promised to give you up his parlor, but if there is any difficulty on that point I promise as a gallant knight to give you the privilege of hanging up on a peg in my closet, whenever it may suit your convenience. . . . We trust therefore to have your Honoress here by the 25th inst, as a living Chirstmas present as large as life, twice as natural & three times as agreable."

It takes time to become part of an intimate group. Though he was now in the coterie, it had been a hard struggle for Mr. Lincoln to make the grade socially at first. He had been just as "blue" during his earlier days in Springfield as he had at Vandalia. He had mentioned it in one of those gloomy letters to Miss Owens written shortly after he arrived: "This thing of living in Springfield is rather a dull business after all, at least it is so to me. I am quite as lonesome here as [I] ever was anywhere in my life. I have been spoken to by but one woman since I've been here, and should not have been by her, if she could have avoided it." There could hardly be a plainer expression of the wish for a woman's sympathy. But he had been timid about seeking occasions and places where he might meet people. He stated his self-doubt plainly: "I've never been to church yet, nor probably shall not be soon. I stay away because I am conscious I should not know how to behave myself."

That not knowing "how to behave" himself in society was the trouble; he was feeling keenly his lack of social and cultural background. He was at home in front of the fireplace of a log cabin, telling droll homey stories that held the attention of all. But being in the sophisticated crowd that gathered in the luxurious parlor of the Edwardses was another matter. Not but what Springfield still had log cabins sprinkled in among the better homes. The combination seems like a symbol of two attitudes which were at war in the little town. On one side was the extreme class consciousness of the age, which seems in some cases like ridiculous snobbery now; on the other the leveling democracy of the near frontier. The perfect representatives of the aristocratic attitude would have been Ninian W. Edwards and his wife; of the second, Abraham Lincoln. This dramatic conflict of ideals was to blow like an icy wind upon the budding love of Abraham and Molly.

One can rarely recover the exact time at which a romance begins. Even the two parties most intimately concerned can seldom put their fingers upon the precise moment at the time and this love story occurred more than a century ago. It is possible to follow the record of Lincoln's outward life in early 1840 but not his inner thoughts and feelings about little Miss Todd.

Mr. Lincoln was busy in the legislature early in the year, attending to public affairs as a good Whig should. There is no doubt he was up to his ears in politics and so were some of his intimate friends. One notes, for example, Joshua Speed's name along with his signed to a campaign circular in January and the signatures include also another person destined to come intimately into this tangled story of a courtship, Dr. Anson G. Henry. This kind-faced physician, five years older than Lincoln, had a warm, sympathetic personality as well as strong Whig convictions. Lincoln loved and depended upon him. Down the long years ahead the skein of his life would cross those of Lincoln and his wife and always there would be understanding and affection among the three.

Lincoln's stream of letters to his absent law partner, John Todd Stuart, kept him in touch with legal and political happenings in Springfield. Occasionally there was a street fight in the red-hot politics of the town. Once the junior partner wrote how the "Little Giant," Stephen A. Douglas, who was a leading Democrat, tried to cane Lincoln's friend Simeon Francis, editor of the Whig *Sangamo Journal*, because Douglas considered himself insulted by something that had been printed in the *Journal*. "Francis caught him by the hair and jammed him back against a market-cart, where the matter ended by Francis being pulled away from him," wrote Lincoln. "The whole affair was so ludicrous that Francis and everybody else (Douglas excepted) have been laughing about it ever since." So much for his light account, but Lincoln before long would find out that politics could involve danger to his own person that was no laughing matter.

The political pot, always bubbling in lively fashion, was boiling furiously in 1840 because it was election year. The Whig candidate was William Henry Harrison, with whom is associated the slogan "Log cabin and hard cider" and that phrase of irresistibly jaunty rhythm "Tippecanoe and Tyler too." It is not possible to separate courtship and politics in this story; they are tangled together.

In March the Sangamon County Whig convention nominated candidates for the legislature. Lincoln was nominated for another term, but Molly's brother-in-law, Mr. Edwards, was not. "Ninian was verry much hurt at not being nominated," wrote Abraham, adding, "I was much, verry much, wounded myself at his being left out." There was unalloyed friendship in the young lawyer's remark, but one wonders, when one considers the feeling of superiority which Ninian and his wife later had toward Lincoln, whether they resented this episode. The Edwardses were always to find it hard to understand why honors came to him. When he was finally nominated for President, some of the family connections met the announcement with shocked unbelief.

In the many letters which Lincoln wrote his partner, Molly's Cousin John, he gives no information as to whether he was seeing much of her. To be sure, he was away from Springfield a good deal that spring, going from town to town to give political speeches or to attend court on the semiannual round of the judicial circuit. Undoubtedly the coterie had its usual gay get-togethers, and they possibly saw each other occasionally at these parties.

Focusing again for a moment on the coterie, one finds a delightful description of a picnic that summer of 1840 in one of James Conkling's letters to Mercy. One of the hostesses for this outing was Anna Rodney and surely, if Mr. Lincoln was in town, he was invited. Today a young man writing his fiancée about a picnic might say briefly that the weather was fine, the food good, and after the lunch they danced. But James presented the subject in Victorian language that made it much more glamorous: " 'Twas really a delightful scene. The branches of some of the tallest trees formed a canopy over our heads to screen us from the rays of a cloudless sun." The lawn, of course, was "velvet" and the table "was loaded with a profusion of delicacies which our ladies know how to prepare so well. The graces flew while daylight lasted and as the dim twilight gathered around us the Graces and the Muses both tripped it 'on the light fantastic toe.' . . ."

With her enthusiasm for the Whig party it would have been the natural thing for Molly to read about the speeches Mr. Lincoln was making in various places in Illinois. She may also have noticed that he had become a member of the board of trustees of the town of Springfield.

He was a rising man and she enjoyed talking with him, but she enjoyed talking to certain other gentlemen too. There was that dynamic Mr. Douglas. A highly gifted personality looked out from those remarkable blue eyes of his. She always delighted in people of talent and intellect. Except that he was not much taller than herself, she considered him a handsome figure and, as she herself said later, she "liked him well enough." But as an ardent Whig, she did not agree with him politically.

A bright-colored story gives a picture of these two on the streets of Springfield, a picture one wishes one could see in a painting. She was sitting on a porch, weaving a wreath of roses, perhaps for decoration for a party or perhaps for the crowning of her own rich hair, when Douglas appeared and asked her to walk with him. Gaily teasing, she agreed on condition he would wear the wreath. Douglas entered into the spirit of the thing, the roses were placed incongruously on that massive and powerful head, and off they went, probably to the accompaniment of girlish giggles.

There may have been times when Molly wondered whether it was her fate to be paired off with a short man. That widower who had signed the plea to Mrs. Browning, Mr. Edwin B. Webb, was far from tall. He was much older than Molly and had two children and he was to make it very clear that he had selected her for his second wife. It is not possible to find out exactly when this romance began either. But it is clear that in the early summer of 1840 Mary Todd was living lightheartedly in the gay, sweet young world of a popular belle with a number of beaux. Just how much her friend Mr. Lincoln figured in her thoughts and whether he had much of a lead over the others at this time is hard to determine.

CHAPTER 5

"My Beaux Have Always Been Hard Bargains"

MOLLY'S eager spirit always delighted in travel and visiting. She had an uncle living in Columbia, Missouri, Judge David Todd, whom she had never seen. Like most of the Todds, he held a substantial position in his community. There was a special attraction in his home in the fact that he had a daughter Anne who was not far from Mary's age. As a Southern girl, Mary had great interest in and loyalty to her relatives and visiting one's kinfolk was in the proper Southern tradition; she would visit Uncle David and Cousin Anne. So she set out for Columbia, Missouri, in the early part of the summer of 1840.

She probably went to St. Louis by stagecoach (a trip of two days or more and a rough one) and there boarded a paddle-wheel steamboat or packet. This would have had to churn its way up the great Mississippi for a short distance, then push into the muddy Missouri River, and continue moving against the current until it reached Boonville or Rocheport. From either town Mary could be taken by horse-drawn conveyance across to Columbia, or she could even have gone on horseback, as she had grown up a good

Kentucky horsewoman. On this trip she undoubtedly had some escort or protector, as young females did not go traveling alone in the eighteen-forties.

While Mary unquestionably liked the opposite sex and had a great deal of coquetry, it speaks well of her personality that she quickly formed affectionate and unselfish friendships with other girls. All her life she was to have deep, devoted friendships with other women. Now she promptly took her cousin Anne Todd to her affectionate heart and they became constant and congenial companions.

Returning for a moment to a survey of Lincoln's day-by-day activities as they have been traced through letters and other contemporary documents, one finds a blank between July 2 and July 13, 1840. A possible explanation is that Lincoln was away from Springfield during that time and this gap may have special significance. A well-defined tradition that has come down among the descendants of Judge David Todd says he came to Columbia to see Molly. One is wary of tradition; it is apt to be affected by hindsight and increase like a rolling snowball as it passes from generation to generation. One must regard it as a court of law does hearsay evidence, seek confirmation of it in contemporary letter or document, and check whether it is consistent with established facts.

Unfortunately the brief visit of an unknown lawyer to a little town in Missouri in 1840 would not have been important enough to be recorded; at least, no contemporary record of it has yet come to light. But the tradition does fit as perfectly as a piece of jigsaw puzzle into the picture formed by otherwise known facts. There is a letter which Molly

wrote from Columbia on July 23 and certain cryptic remarks in it leap into meaning if one accepts this tradition.
Also the period of Lincoln's apparent absence from Springfield makes the timing correct.

The time element enables one to throw out one detail
which has been attached to this story. It has been said the
occasion of Mr. Lincoln's coming up the Missouri River
was a great Whig rally at Rocheport. There was such a
rally between June 18 and 20, 1840, but turning to the
record of Lincoln's day-by-day existence, it is found he
appeared in court at Springfield on June 18 and signed a
document there on June 22. If this is the rally meant, he
could hardly, under the slow conditions of travel by steamboat and horsepower, have had time to make the trip and
return between those dates. The tradition had it that he
came to Rocheport on business. Perhaps somewhere along
the line of the tradition's transmission someone thought the
rally made a most plausible reason for such a good Whig as
Lincoln to come to Missouri, put two and two together and
got five. But this in no way conflicts with the basic family
tradition that Mr. Lincoln came to Columbia to see Molly,
which does fit into the known facts.

This family story says that he went to the Presbyterian
church with Molly the Sunday he was in Columbia, sitting
in the Todd family pew. One likes to let one's imagination
play on the idea of those two figures sitting side by side in
a little church near the frontier — the tall lawyer whose
earnest rugged face perhaps showed a little of the uncertainty and self-consciousness of a man who is courting but
whose gray eyes when they rested on the uplifted, bon-

neted face at his side had a special light in them; and Molly, sweetly reverent, her vivacity hushed in devout worship. It could have done much to bring them close together, to deepen a dawning love, that sitting side by side in the little church contemplating the serious meanings of life.

And now at long last Molly can speak for herself. She wrote from her uncle's home in Columbia a long letter which still exists, a confidential letter glowing with personality, giving an account of the gay happenings in which she was taking part. It also contains certain shy, intriguing hints about topics of deeper import. It is possible to go into the thoughts and feelings of Mary Todd as she herself set them down on the twenty-third day of July in the year 1840. The nearest one can get to a personality of the past is to read the letters of that person. Here Mary talks to one naturally, unrestrainedly, and directly; there is no intermediary and no long stretch of decades between.

The letter was to that beloved friend Mercy Levering with whom she had spent so many intimate and companionable hours during the past winter. Mercy had recently left what Molly called "these western wilds" to return to her home in the East. Molly's heart was desolate at the loss of her running mate; the letter is filled with overflowing affection as well as being a narrative of her activities. What would she do without her "Dearest Merce" when she returned to Springfield?

Molly's happy and responsive spirit viewed scenes and people in Technicolor. Her time had "been most delightfully spent," the Missouri country was "most beautiful," and never had she "encountered more kindness & hospi-

tality." The day before, she and her cousin Anne had "returned from a most agreeable excursion to Boonville, situated immediately on the river and a charming place. We
remained a week, attended four parties, during the time."

There is a suggestion of the small-town girl's liking for
larger horizons and more pomp and circumstance as she
writes that one party "was *particularly* distinguished for
its brilliancy & *city like* doings." The dancing lasted "with
untiring vigor" until three o'clock in the morning (though
she and Cousin Anne left earlier) and the tempo was so
fast and furious that she "felt exhausted after such *desperate
exertions* to keep pace with the music." Apparently Springfield did not hurry through the figures in such "rapid manner," the speeding up of the dancing seemed to change
gracefulness into jerkiness, and Molly saw the funny side
of the spectacle. She expressed her amusement to Mercy in
the stilted language which was then popular: "*Your risibles*
would have undergone a *considerable state* of *excitement*,
were you to have seen the 'poetry of motion' exercised in
the dance." Later in the letter she made a further remark
about happenings to which she seemed unaccustomed and
she showed that even then Illinoisans had their present-day
nickname: "Our Sucker friends would have opened their
orbs, at such strange doings."

In writing she also incidentally revealed her awareness of
the Southern antecedents of her relatives and friends.
Speaking of the music for the dance, she continued thought-
fully: "Had our grandfathers been present in the festive
halls of mirth, they would undoubtedly have recognized the
familiar airs of their youthful days, all the old Virginia

reels that have been handed down to us by *tradition*, were played."

There was no doubt she was having a glorious time on her visit. Molly had that most appealing quality, the gift of natural and contagious enjoyment; to be with her was to share in her pleasure as one does with a happy child. Her enthusiasms were as ever-present as the underscored words in her letters. She loved Missouri. She would love to live in Boonville. "A life on the river to me has always had a charm, so much excitement, and this *you* have deemed necessary to my well being; every day experience impresses me more fully with the belief."

There was a vogue at that time for soul searching and for writing letters in which one analyzed and moralized over one's emotions. Mr. Lincoln is to have a heavy dose of such torturing introspection in the progress of this story. Innocent enjoyment of life was apt to be labeled wicked frivolity in the eighteen-forties and conscientious Mercy Levering had evidently scolded Molly about her lightheartedness.

The letter becomes introspective and gives a hint that something is causing the writer to think seriously about the future and what she wants in that future. It could be that Mr. Lincoln had come to Columbia and Molly had realized that here was a suitor who was in earnest and she must face a far-reaching decision. She had been taking stock of her own qualities. She was sorry she loved excitement and parties so much. "I would such were not my nature, for mine I fancy is to be a quiet lot and happy indeed will I be, if it is, only cast near those, I *so dearly love*." She was seeing clearly here: all her life, affection, both the giving and receiving of it, was to be the most important thing. There is also a hint that already her heart was inclining toward the impecunious Mr. Lincoln. If she was pondering thoughts of becoming his bride, the prospect seemed to of- fer "a quiet lot" indeed.

She continued her self-analysis with a sort of realization that sooner or later her soaring young spirit would have to come down to earth. And, after all, gaieties did not com- pletely satisfy her. "My feelings & hopes are all so san- guine that in this dull world of reality tis best to dispell our delusive day dreams as soon as possible. Would it were in my power to follow your kind advice, my ever dear Merce and turn my thoughts from earthly vanities, to one higher than us all. Every day proves the fallacy of our enjoy- ments, & that we are living for pleasures that do not recom- pense us for the pursuit."

Molly turned for a moment to the subject of the letters and newspapers that had followed her from Springfield, a flood of mail that is good evidence of her popularity. The arrival of the mail, she says prettily, finds her "on the wing of expectation." Knowing her intense interest in the po- litical campaign, some of her friends or beaux had been sending her the local newspapers, the *Sangamo Journal*, the *Old Soldier* (the Whig campaign newspaper), and some daring person had even sent a Democratic newspa- per, probably the campaign one called *Old Hickory*. "This latter," continued Molly, "rather astonished your friend, *there* I had deemed myself forgotten." Did that italicized *"there"* refer by any chance to Mr. Douglas?

Having played around the bush for a number of pages, Molly reached, via the topic of mail, the most intriguing part of her letter: "When I mention *some letters* I have received since leaving S—— you will be somewhat surprised, as I *must confess* they were entirely *unlooked for*." Could Mr. Lincoln have written her? She plainly had a far-reaching matter on her mind and longed for a confidante but was afraid to commit too much to paper. She continued: "This is *between ourselves*, my dearest, but of this more anon. Every day I am convinced this is a stranger world we live in, the *past* as the future is to me a mystery." If only Merce were with her so she could talk to her: "How much I wish you were near, ever have I found yours a congenial heart. In your presence I have almost *thought aloud*, and the thought that paineth most is, that such may never be again. . . ."

Her mood lightened and she returned to her spicy account of events and persons. One is pleased to find a couple of puns, although rather anemic ones, and a bit of the slang of more than a century ago. Molly, partly because of her intense interest in all the people she knew, enjoyed a bit of feminine gossip. Her tongue was rather too apt at ticking off the foibles of her friends. One cannot get the full implication of her comment that one "Martha Jane" now has "an opportunity of making *dead sets* at the youngsters," but one suspects it was a remark that Martha Jane would not have appreciated. Then followed the first of her puns: "To change our subject to one of a *still warmer* nature, did you ever feel such oppressive weather as we have had of late. . . ."

After many pages Molly wrote that Cousin Anne "wonders what I am scribbling so much about." Apropos of the length of the letter came the second pun: "Though I can fancy you pale and exhausted — so in Mercy will spare you." In various letters it is found that Mercy had to put up with considerable punning on her name. Even her fiancé liked to tease her by saying "Oh Mercy!"

But there was one more thing she must tell Merce, because it was on the ever-absorbing subject of beaux. One suspects she made a wry little grimace as she wrote: "There is *one* being here, who cannot brook the mention of my return, an agreeable lawyer & grandson of *Patrick Henry — what an honor!* I shall never survive it — I wish you could see him, the most perfect original I ever met." Then came another statement which might have hidden meaning: "My beaux have *always* been *hard bargains* at any rate." Did Mercy know that young Mr. Lincoln was wont to use that expression "hard bargain" even as his backwoods father had done before him? The young lawyer was to be regarded by Mary's relatives in Springfield as matrimonially a "hard bargain" for the eligible belle that she was. There is great significance in the comment on Patrick Henry's descendant which follows: "Uncle and others think, he surpasses his *noble ancestor* in *talents*, yet Merce I love him not, & my hand will never be given, where my heart is not." Molly could have come far enough in her romance with Mr. Lincoln to know that love and congeniality should be the essential elements in the marriage she might make in that mysterious future. Sometimes it takes the beginning of genuine love to bestow that bit of wisdom.

CHAPTER 6

Various Happenings of a Romantic Nature

THE rest of the summer and up to November of 1840 Lincoln was in and out of Springfield helping elect President Harrison by making political speeches over the state and attending to his legal duties on the fall round of the judicial circuit. Then the meeting of the legislature late in November kept him at home. Mary too was deeply absorbed in the political campaign, though she had a guilty feeling about it. After the election she wrote Merce: "I suppose like the rest of us *Whigs* . . . you have been rejoicing in the recent election of Gen Harrison," and continued rather apologetically: "This fall I became quite a *politician*, rather an unladylike profession. . . ." She excused herself on the ground that the cause was "one of such vital importance to our prosperity," and it was a time of "*crisis.*"

The two girls were in a dilemma about their interest in politics. Such interest was genuine in a matter which so vitally concerned the gentlemen of their thoughts, but to be considered unwomanly by these same gentlemen would be dreadful. Perhaps politics had a special fascination because it was forbidden fruit. Mercy, who was the soul of propriety, wrote her fiancé late that fall, making her attitude plain. She mentioned listening to speeches "upon a subject which the narrow capabilities of my sex can understand but little," but she felt that women should not "be totally ignorant of the great, and important questions pending upon the government of her own happy country." Lest that statement be considered too radical she continued: "But by engaging her mind in the things that belong exclusively to your sex she is liable to become perplexed and bewildered in thing[s] that are incompatible with the more retired sphere of usefulness which a kind and beneficent Providence has seen fit in his all wise disposal to allot to her. So soon as she goes beyond that sphere she does I *think* lose her dependence and ceases to be the amiable, and attractive creature she is sometimes called." That statement should have convinced young Mr. Conkling that he was in no danger of marrying a strong-minded female.

Peeping further into the private correspondence of these delightful Victorian sweethearts and going back to the month of September, one finds James Conkling reporting that he saw Molly after her return from Missouri. "It was on a Saturday evening at the [Sangamo] Journal Office where some fifteen or twenty ladies were collected together to listen to the Tippecanoe Singing Club." If Mr. Lincoln was in town, it is a safe guess that he was there. It is evident what a social and political center that little newspaper office just off the square was, as Mr. Conkling continued: "It has become lately quite a place of resort, particularly when it is expected there will be any speeches." The subject of speeches being thus gracefully introduced, he told his fiancée the really important item in this passage: "I had the honor of being called on myself that evening and made a few brief remarks."

But Mr. Conkling had a topic even more interesting to an engaged couple. He seems to have been a popular groomsman at weddings, just as Mary Todd was a frequent bridesmaid. "Well," wrote James to Mercy, "I had no idea I should ever be instrumental more than once again, in changing the name of a lady. But last evening Miss Todd and myself, (standing partners you perceive) with the assistance of Parson Bergen in his usual dignified manner passed through the usual ceremonies of such an occasion." He told how, about ten o'clock, he and Miss Todd helped pack the newlyweds, Mr. and Mrs. Sidney Abell, into a stagecoach and sent them off to Chicago. "Peace and Happiness be with them," was his benediction.

James Conkling walked home with Molly after the wedding. A girl needed an escort at night in Springfield. There were no street lights and only an occasional window square was dimly lit by candlelight or oil lamp. One was like as not to stumble over a pig.

The two young people strolled along the well-known path that crossed a little bridge and led up the hill to the Edwards mansion. Next door to it stood the home of Mercy's brother, to which James had so often seen Mercy herself home after a party. He wanted to talk of her to Molly; they both missed her so much. He did very well in putting his lover's longing into his letter: "The same heavenly stars shone . . . but not your bright and starry eyes — the same gurgl[ing] of the brook, was heard, but I listened in vain for the tones of your silvery voice. The light streamed from your brother's window . . . but it did not guide me to your presence. And for the first time, I think, I accompanied a lady home, upon that hill, without having the satisfaction of reflecting upon my return that it was yourself." This lover well deserved his nickname of "Jacob Faithful."

In contrast to this nostalgic mood he gave a gay and teasing description of his "blooming partner [at the wedding] who has just returned from Missouri." Alas for Mary, all that abundant hospitality she had so enjoyed on her visit had increased her weight! He made the most in humorous fashion of that fact: "Verily, I believe the further West a young lady goes the better her health becomes. If she comes here she is sure to grow — if she visits Missouri she will soon grow out of your recollection and if she should visit the Rocky Mountains I know not what would become of her." But for all his teasing he had a fellow feeling with Miss Todd, who like himself regretted Mercy's absence so much and felt so lonesome.

As always in a young part of the country there was much marrying and giving in marriage. Bachelors in large numbers, as a rhyme of the day said, were being "strung in Hymen's noose." Miss Todd is found attending another wedding less than a month later — that of James Campbell and Harriet Huntington. She was the only lady present unconnected with the family. Her liveliness and warm interest undoubtedly made her a welcome addition to any wedding occasion. James Conkling, of course, wrote Mercy about it. Meantime he had had an answer from her, apparently, warning him about the danger of officiating at so many weddings, for he replied: "And so you thought that a word of caution might be necessary for me for if Miss T. and myself were partners much oftener, we might stand up once too often." But another girl had been his partner on this occasion and apparently a very attractive one too, for he teasingly asked Mercy what she would think if she knew that he had been "subjected to a very strong temptation" to follow the groom's "most brilliant example," had he not, he added tenderly, "been under the influence of a power more firm than destiny."

So much for scraps of mention, mere side glimpses, of Mary in ancient, yellowing letters. Sometime in the latter half of 1840 young Conkling might have written his fiancée some very interesting news that was getting around: that Mr. Lincoln was frequently seen among the other young hopefuls adorning the slippery horsehair sofas in the Edwards parlor, that he, as well as Edwin B. Webb, was paying particular court to Miss Todd. It could be noticed that Mr. Lincoln was not calling her "Miss Todd" any more but was using the nickname that somehow seemed to suit her, "Molly." One can imagine some member of the romantic-minded and Shakespeare-quoting coterie that fall suddenly assuming a knowing expression and saying: " 'Sits the wind in that corner?' Has Mr. Lincoln fallen in love with Molly?"

Elizabeth Edwards, experienced in such matters, before long became aware of what was taking place. She began to notice the expression on Mr. Lincoln's face when he looked at Mary. Elizabeth would enter the room where the girl was entertaining her caller and mark with an older sister's keen appraisal how the young lawyer sat listening to the girl as if hypnotized — his eyes glued on her glowing and expressive face. Her letters show how much of interest the younger sister had to tell and how well she told it and it is easy to accept Elizabeth Edwards's statement that Mr. Lincoln "was charmed with Mary's wit and fascinated with her quick sagacity — her will — her nature — and culture." When this sparkling flow of conversation was delivered in a soft voice with a decided Southern accent, and with pretty little gestures, and dimples that came and went, Mr. Lincoln found the effect irresistible.

He did not have much to say himself, according to Elizabeth's account; he "could not hold a lengthy conversation with a lady — was not sufficiently educated & intelligent in the female line to do so." One wonders whether there was special emphasis on the word "lady." Before Mary came to live in Springfield and for a time afterwards, Mrs. Edwards had done her hospitable duty in regard to her husband's colleague in the legislature. But the time was approaching when the hospitable attitude at the Edwards home would cease. At some point Elizabeth Edwards, perhaps becoming better informed about Mr. Lincoln's poverty and hard-scrabble beginnings, began to wear a disapproving expression.

But wooing was going on with Mr. Lincoln's calls that fall at the Edwards home on the hill. He and Mary undoubtedly met and had their moments at the coterie's continual round of parties and outings. In that slow-motion age before automobiles, telephones, or moving pictures, courting couples in Springfield took long walks together on the black and overgrown paths that wound their way out from the straggling town into the edge of the prairie. It was a prairie that bloomed with countless flowers in season and gathering these provided a wonderful objective for two young people who wished to be together.

Again those subsidiary lovers, James and Mercy, give a close-up view. Young Conkling was writing his fiancée that fall of 1840: "I . . . recollected those happy hours when we strolled together on the prairies when arrayed in all their splendor and decked with the gaudy hues of summer. . . ." So full was the assortment of blossoms that in another letter he mentioned gathering thirty varieties. He continued, loverwise: ". . . and I looked forward to those still more happy hours, when I trust we may wind our paths across those same prairies, under a clear and cloudless sky and regaled by the fragrance of their millions of flowers."

So it may well have been that Mr. Lincoln and Molly walked together on the prairie that fall, finding companionship and congeniality and thinking of a future in which that companionship would become permanent. If the paths were ankle-deep in mud or dust, it did not matter in that radiant and iridescent world which surrounds two young people falling in love.

James Conkling, devoted fiancé that he was, had withdrawn from society and may have been slow in becoming aware of Lincoln's shy courting. Other personalities and events in the latter part of 1840 were much more in the public eye. The gossips very likely were speculating about whether Miss Todd would become Mrs. Webb or Mrs. Douglas. They all knew that Mr. Webb was courting her and he was a man of experience in such matters, being, as Mary herself put it, "a widower of modest merit." In December, writing Merce of doings in the coterie, she mentioned that Mr. Webb "is our *principal lion*, [and] dances attendance very frequently."

The "Little Giant," Stephen A. Douglas, was also in evidence. He was quite a ladies' man, skillful in the little attentions dear to their hearts and master of give-and-take in banter and jest. His dramatic and self-assured presence was apt socially to eclipse that of the slow, unobtrusive, and sometimes wistful Lincoln.

It could have been about this time that one of Mary's friends asked her pointedly which she "intended to have," Lincoln or Douglas. The girl turned aside such undue inquisitiveness with a light answer: "Him who has the best prospects of being President." It has been said that a fortuneteller once predicted she would marry a future President and any buoyant girl would like to dwell on that pleasant subject. (After she was married, her boundless faith in her husband made her predict his future greatness in earnest, even to the point of sometimes embarrassing him.) Literal-minded biographers of Lincoln later interpreted this parrying remark as a statement of cold-blooded, scheming ambition, building up a case against an affectionate woman who was asking only at this time that her lot be "cast near those, I *so dearly love*."

In November, Mary, still lonesome for Mercy Levering, joyfully welcomed a new companion. The stagecoach brought from Alton a pretty, sparkling, conscientious girl of eighteen, Matilda Edwards, a cousin of Ninian's, to spend the winter at the Edwards home. Molly had undoubtedly made the last part of her return trip from Missouri by just such a journey as Matilda's and one is now able to get a close-up view of the ruggedness of stagecoach travel.

Matilda wrote her brother a short time after she reached Springfield that she had had a hard trip with two overnight stops. "The first day was the most unpleasant one I ever passed," ran her account. "Crowded as I was up in one corner with the weight of all three of the gentlemen upon me as I supposed you can immagine what I really suffered. When we alighted for the night I was quite lame." To make matters worse, one of the three gentlemen who formed her abundant masculine escort was a suitor, Mr. Strong, so in spite of discomfort, as she said: ". . . I was compelled through the day to *sit looking* and *acting my very prettiest* which you know was to me a *difficult* task." She was evidently successful in her endeavor, for she added at once: "Mr S was very agreeable as you may suppose."

Stopping overnight at inns where one was lucky to have a room to oneself often had its element of the unexpected. Matilda's sprightly narrative continued: "The first night we stopped I had a very nice room to myself with the exception that the floor above was rather too thin for one of my glib tongue. As soon as the gentleman retired the landlady came in and I to win her good will, exclaimed '*what dirty creatures these men are they have spit all over your nice floor.*'" This speech Mr. Strong "had the kindness to repeat to me the next morning which of course was *very mortifying.* . . ."

Travel on the second day proved much more comfortable than on the first "and when we halted for the night," wrote Matilda, "I was in so fine a humor, that either *for this* or some other reason I was supposed to be a young wife taking a bridal tour. The good landlady and all her household had very Strong suspicions." It seems to have been an age of punning.

At Ninian's home Matilda and Mary were delighted with each other from the first. The newcomer wrote her brother at once that Mary Todd was "a very lovely and sprightly girl." Within a month Mary was writing enthusiastically to Mercy about Matilda as her welcome companion, "a congenial spirit I assure you . . . a lovelier girl I never saw." Matilda referred to "dear Molly" in her letters, but one can only guess that Mary used her friend's appealing nickname "Tid." It was a devoted friendship that was to last to the end of Matilda's too brief life.

Of course the arrival of an attractive and eligible girl "on the hill" created quite a stir among what Mary called the *"marriageable gentlemen"* in the coterie. In no time at all the susceptible Joshua Speed, to use her words, was offering his "ever changing heart" and *"young* affections" at Matilda's shrine. Judging from certain references in Mr. Lincoln's letters to Speed later, it is likely that this new devotion resulted in quite a heartache for sixteen-year-old Sarah Rickard, sister-in-law to Lincoln's friend William Butler. Sarah had apparently looked too much upon Joshua's handsome and romantic countenance and had fallen in love with him.

The crosscurrents of love affairs in the coterie, as always with a group of young people at the marrying age, were complicated. When these affairs were occurring simultaneously with Abraham's wooing of Mary, the record was likely to become mixed up. Sarah's name has at times been pulled, somewhat ridiculously, into the story of Lincoln's courtship.

Sarah lived for a time with her sister, Mrs. William Butler, at whose home Lincoln was a boarder and later also a roomer. Sarah herself said afterwards she regarded him as an older brother, just as the Butler children did. He liked to play with them, as he did with all children, and to delight their young imaginations with whimsical remarks. One day he teasingly told Sarah that since in the Bible Abraham married Sarah and since his name was Abraham and hers Sarah, the logical conclusion seemed to be that they should be married. Again a light statement has been repeated with cold seriousness in later years by those who had lost the playful setting. The result was an impression that Lincoln had proposed marriage in earnest to a girl with whom he was only being playful and whom he undoubtedly regarded as a mere child.

"We see a great deal of company," wrote Matilda shortly after her arrival. Mary mentioned that "some others" in addition to Joshua were much attracted to the visiting girl. Within two months gossiping tongues of Springfield were speculating about Mr. Lincoln's feeling toward this new charmer, whose gaiety and humor in her recently found letters peep shyly out through the heavy sense of duty which oppressed her.

Matilda, like so many of these letter writers, was much concerned with the state of her soul. As was the case with

Mercy Levering, she did not wish to indulge in wicked frivolity. "I have received an invitation to a ball since I came,"
she wrote, "but of course did not accept it. No my brother
however inconsistant my life may be as a christians I hope I
shall ever have strength to resist those worldly fascinations
which if indulged in bring a reproach upon the cause of
religion."

Ninian, eying his pretty young cousin, urged her to go,
saying she "would appear to advantage" at the ball and using other arguments likely to appeal to eighteen-year-old
femininity. But Matilda could not be shaken from her lofty
resolutions. Congenial as she and Mary were, they evidently
did not agree about balls and dancing, and presumably
Molly went gaily to the party while Matilda stayed at home
wrapped in virtuous thoughts.

Since lively young Springfield is in effect one of our
dramatis personae, one should perhaps, before laying Matilda's letter aside, notice her impressions of the town. Before leaving Alton she had looked forward enthusiastically
to visiting the wonderful new state capital. "You are I suppose," she wrote her brother, "anxious to know how the
city which haunted both my daily and nightly dreams appears when divested of all except reality. The truth that
'distance lends enchantment to the view' is now . . . fully
realized. Alton has doubled in attractions while this garden
of Eden is fast losing the charms with which my fancy
decked it. The . . . dazling mantle woven by your imag-
inative sister finds not the wearer in the fascinations of
Springfield."

The raw aspect of the town gave some newcomers that

Two Important Structures in Springfield

Above, home of Mr. and Mrs. Ninian W. Edwards as it appeared at a later period. The porch was not there at the time Abraham courted Mary. *Below*, Illinois State Capitol in public square. This view from the west side, taken probably in 1859, is very much the same view Lincoln saw daily from his abode over Speed's store. At the far right is the American House, where the "Cotillion Party" took place.

Pertinent Information from Mr. Lincoln and Mary

Mary writes Mrs. Gideon Welles (December 6, 1865) that Mr. Lincoln often told her, both before and after marriage, that she was the only woman he had ever cared for.

Mr. Lincoln writes Joshua Speed (July 4, 1842) that he has decided to stand
still and let the Lord direct him in his tangled love affair.

Godey's Lady's Book, November 18

Proper Attire for a Wedding?

The latest style at the time of the wedding. Mary's dress was undoubtedly fashioned on such lines.

Courtesy of the Chicago Historical Socie

Proper Attire for a Dance

Detail of a men's fashion plate of 1837. The costumes at the cotillion in 1839 would have been very similar to these. Notice the long sideburns and compare with Mr. Lincoln's in frontispiece.

impression at first until they became acquainted with its neighborly people. Matilda finished her letter some days later and toward the close of it referred to her "first impressions" on arrival and then continued: "But since then I can say that a change has come over the spirit of my dreams. I am now beginning to like Springfield and enjoy myself very much."

Early in December, Mary and Matilda doubtless heard much chatter about a rather comical incident in the legislature. That body, the state house being not yet ready for its sessions, was meeting in a church. For party reasons the Whigs wished to prevent an adjournment and therefore did not want a quorum to be present to vote on the matter. Most of the Whigs accordingly stayed away, but Lincoln and a couple of his friends, overconfident, attended the session to see what was going on. When a roll call was taken and to their great surprise a quorum was announced, they were filled with dismay and hastily made an exit through the window. The meeting being on the ground floor of the church, the feat was not difficult for a person with Lincoln's long legs, but of course it was too late to prevent the adjournment. The undignified departure accomplished nothing except to arouse the glee and sarcasm of the Democrats. Their newspaper, the *Illinois State Register*, suggested that the state house be raised another story so that Mr. Lincoln, even with his long legs, when he wished to make such an exit, would have to climb down the water spout!

It is no wonder the episode was a painful subject to Mr.

Lincoln afterwards. It is a hard thing for a man struggling to rise out of humble beginnings and to make a place for himself to be put in a ridiculous position. It has already been seen how the affair with Miss Owens wounded his pride. The years centering around Lincoln's courtship of Mary Todd were to involve the most searing humiliations and one of the deepest depressions of his life.

CHAPTER 7

"Crime of Matrimony"

F OR the fall months of 1840 there are only a few casual references to Molly. But in December it is possible to stand confidently upon a broad expanse of solid evidence, a long letter which she herself wrote Mercy Levering.

Molly, the lively conversationalist, can be counted upon to give all the current news and bring things up to date. Here is a good narrative of happenings from the best source possible. But as to certain thoughts in her mind she is not so forthright; she merely throws in some tantalizing hints.

It has been "very many weary days" since she had heard from her "ever dear Merce." Molly apologized for not answering her friend's last letter sooner, but she and Mrs. Edwards had been busy for several weeks in the fall with "a formidable supply of *sewing*, necessary to winter comfort." The last words conjure up visions of flannel petticoats and allied underthings, for houses heated only with stoves and open fires are cold. Sewing was underscored in the life of most women in those days when one could not buy clothes ready-made, as now. Molly could not foresee how much of it fate had in store for her in the next twenty years: baby clothes, patches for little boys' pants, and dresses to make herself pretty for her husband and bring a light to his eyes.

After the fall sewing, the social whirl, which Matilda had mentioned, began. Again Molly described Matilda with great enthusiasm: "A most interesting young lady, her fascinations, have drawn a concourse of beaux & company round us." She piled up her praises of the visiting girl and her affection for her without any signs of jealousy.

The legislature being in session, bringing what Molly described as "birds of passage," she continued: "We expect a very gay winter, evening before last my sister gave a most agreeable party, upwards of a hundred graced the festive scene." Mr. Lincoln was probably among the dressed-up gentlemen who climbed the hill that evening and perhaps a certain gathering storm was already making itself evident in a few preliminary flashes of disapproval in Mrs. Edwards's eyes.

But Mary was seeing him frequently. She went on to tell Mercy of a pleasant jaunt that she was looking forward to very much. A little group led by Mr. Hardin and Mr. Browning and including Matilda and herself, Mr. Webb, and Mr. Lincoln was going to Jacksonville to spend a day or two. She added longingly: "We are watching the clouds most anxiously trusting it may snow, so we may have a sleigh ride. — Will it not be pleasant?" It is at least pleasant to contemplate such a sleighload of interesting people, to picture Molly with her red cheeks and vibrant joyousness and Mr. Lincoln slow and deliberate with his face perhaps lighted by a whimsical twinkle. That expedition opened up distinct possibilities for stolen moments between two lovers and it could be that much of importance took place on it.

Mary gave the local news. The state house was not yet

completed but sufficiently so to allow the legislature to meet within its walls. From other sources it is known that two days after Lincoln stepped out of the convenient window of the church which had been the meeting place, the august body did meet in the state house.

"Springfield has improved astonishingly," she continued, "[we] have the addition of another *bell* to the Second Church. It rings so long & loud, that as in days past we cannot mistake the trysting hour." One likes to imagine here the tones of those church bells of a Sunday morning ringing out over the scattered homes calling to worship the quaintly dressed ladies and gentlemen of more than a century ago. Among them one can picture Mary in her best bonnet and billowy skirt hurrying down the hill and across the bridge to enter the church door and sit among her friends. Her religion, her belief in the goodness of God, was unquestioning and church was to her a place of comfort and peace. The time would come when, as the President's lady, she would write back to Springfield in homesick fashion, asking that "*our particular pew*," in which she and her husband had sat for many years, would be theirs again when they returned.

Mercy had written in her last "kind, soul cheering epistle" to Mary that "time has borne changes on its wing." In answer Mary reported on these changes in men's attire; certain gentlemen had been getting new clothes: "Speed's 'grey suit' has gone the way of *all flesh*, an interesting suit of *Harrison blues* have replaced his *sober livery, Lincoln's lincoln green* have gone to dust. . . ." Mr. Webb, in spite of his courting, wore something to indicate he was in mourning.

Naturally, Molly reported the state of Mercy's pining fiancé, who "seems to have *given up all*, when deprived of his 'own particular star.' " She, Molly, had not seen him for a good chat since they walked home together after attending the Abell wedding in September. She added with friendly concern: "I have often wished for the sake of his society & of your *dear self* he would be more social." This passage served to introduce the topic of marriages and Mary seized the opportunity to expand on it. Evidently it was a subject which was very much occupying her thoughts.

Her letter gave a report of the two autumn brides whose weddings she had attended. Harriet Campbell, married in October, "appears to be enjoying all the sweets of married life," but Martha Jane Abell, September bride, was not seen about very much and "her *silver tones*, the other evening were not quite so captain like as was their wont in former times." Mary asked a very thoughtful question: "Why is it that married folks always become so serious?"

Another friend of them both, it was rumored, was soon to be married, continued Mary. "I am pleased she is about perpetrating the *crime* of *matrimony* . . . I think she will be much happier." Did this peculiar choice of the word "crime" have any connection with what her family were saying about a marriage which she was contemplating? Something was worrying Mary. She was losing weight: "I still am the same ruddy *pineknot*, only not quite so great an exuberance of flesh, as it once was my lot to contend with, although quite a sufficiency." The words "ruddy pineknot" suggest her warm coloring and her glowing health and vitality.

Apparently Mercy had been counseling her friend again to think more solemn thoughts. Molly answered: "You bid me pause, in your last, on the banks of *'Lionel'* & there glean a useful lesson, by marking the changes, the destroying hand of time has written on all." ("Lionel" seems to be the name the girls used in referring to the little stream whose bridge one crossed on the way downtown from the hill; more matter-of-fact citizens commonly referred to it as "Town Branch.") Standing in imagination beside the brook, as Mercy had directed, Molly gave her instinct for poetic expression full fling: "The icy hand of winter has set its seal upon the waters, the winds of Heaven visit the spot but roughly, the same stars shine down, yet not with the same liquid, mellow light as in the olden time. Some forms & memories that enhanced the place, have passed by. . . ."

Toward the end of this lengthy letter, in apologizing for the behavior of her "stump of a pen," she used an expression found often in her letters and one showing a certain characteristic: "Pass my imperfections lightly as usual, I throw myself on your amiable nature, knowing that my shortcomings will be forgiven." She could with confidence have said these same words in her future married life to her indulgent husband. But one day, as First Lady of the land, she would find that the public does not pass imperfections lightly by.

Molly's letter was written around the middle of Decem-

ber 1840; she did not give the exact day. It is known that
by the end of that month, before the catastrophe of January 1, 1841, certain events and emotional experiences had
taken place. The attraction between Mary and Mr. Lincoln had grown stronger and stronger and had revealed to
them increasingly important discoveries of pleasure and satisfaction in each other's company.

To Molly the rugged face that Springfield called homely
had grown more and more dear until it had become the one
face in the world that mattered most. For her there was tenderness around the sensitive mouth and a special light in
the earnest gray eyes. Mrs. Edwards, experienced matchmaker that she was, had diagnosed that look: "Mr. Lincoln
loved Mary."

He had diagnosed his feeling himself. He is shortly to tell
of a certain test he had thought out to determine whether
a gentleman was in love with a girl and he had evidently
applied it. This was definitely the girl with whom he wished
to plod life through hand in hand. He may have wondered
how he ever could have thought that about Miss Owens.
How pallid his feeling toward her had been, compared to
the vitality of this attraction. Life would seem less plodding with the companionship of Molly, so joyous and intensely alive.

This was an age when fathers and guardians had much
to say about the marriage of a girl, when they had certain
heavy-handed rights in the matter. A proper gentleman of
the period, when his intentions became serious, must ask
permission to pay his addresses to the lady of his choice.
Ninian Edwards considered that Mary Todd, living under

his roof in Springfield, was his ward. But apparently Mr. Lincoln took the approach of writing Mary's father, Mr. Robert S. Todd, at Lexington instead of consulting Mary's brother-in-law. Whereupon Mr. Todd wrote Ninian asking about this Mr. Abraham Lincoln and whether he was qualified to become the husband of Mary Todd. Knowing Ninian's settled aristocratic notions, one speculates about his reply.

Of course the many reasons why Lincoln was not in a position to marry which he had so painstakingly pointed out to Miss Owens still existed. Molly, unused to hard work, accustomed to luxurious living, to the assurance that comes from prominent connections, Molly, who loved the trimmings of life and took the essentials (for which he was still struggling) for granted, whose family considered their aristocracy more or less a divine right, was not the logical choice for him. He was shortly to remember all these factors with intense force. He was to state later with the voice of experience that reason has nothing to do with falling in love, that it is a matter of the heart and not the head, of the appeal of a girl's personality and her bright eyes. Swept away by the most powerful emotion of a young man's life, Lincoln became engaged to Mary Todd.

It is remarkable how these lovers managed to leave a record in their own words of their feeling and attitude toward marriage. It was a subject to which, first and last, they gave deep consideration. They were not in their impulsive teens. Mary at the end of 1840 had just had her twenty-second birthday and Lincoln was within less than two months of his thirty-second. What did Mary say about marriage?

It has been seen that she declined the descendant of Patrick Henry because she did not love him and she would not marry a man she did not love. She is soon to tell of her refusing another earnest suitor because, as she said, he was not congenial and she would not marry a man with whom she was not congenial.

Most important of all was her clear-cut statement that she "would rather marry a good man — a man of mind — with a hope and bright prospects ahead" than marry all the wealth and gold in the world. There is no trace here of the class consciousness of the Edwardses. For Mary the requirements in a husband were goodness, brains, congeniality, and love. In this she stepped into the fundamental democratic American attitude on which the nation prides itself today.

What was Lincoln's approach to marriage? A small pointer is in that self-mocking account of his courtship of Miss Owens: once a woman was his wife, he said, he would use all his powers "in search of perfections in her, which might be fairly set-off against her defects." This is a wholesome attitude as far as it goes, but there is something more far-reaching in the advice he was before long to give to a friend who had just acquired a wife: "You owe obligations to her, ten thousand times more sacred than any you can owe to others; and in that light, let them be respected and observed."

Another clue, though not from his own pen, is in a book which Lincoln is said to have marked and presented to his wife later. The book exists today and one finds among the marked passages one on marriage: "This union, so sacred that it even supercedes that which exists between parent and child, should be entered upon only from the highest and purest motives."

But the most appealing evidence of Lincoln's approach to his marriage lies in the words he chose to have engraved in the wedding ring he was finally to place upon the hand of his bride.

It is not known at what time the two became engaged, what tender words were spoken between them, or with what touch of arms and lips the agreement was sealed. These were two people of warm, affectionate natures. Very soon there will be a close-up view of Lincoln gathering the girl into his arms, seating her on his lap as if she were a child, and kissing away her tears. The promptness with which he took these measures may indicate it was not the first time he had employed them.

The details of their formal troth are hidden. One knows only that when the New Year of 1841 was welcomed in, Mary and Abraham had confessed their love to each other, were engaged, and were planning to be married.

CHAPTER 8

He Was "Mr. Lincoln" to Her

WHAT did Mary Todd see in this Mr. Lincoln to whom she had just become engaged? He was always "Mr. Lincoln" to her until in time she would call him "Father" to their children. It was not her habit to address him as "Abe" or "Abraham"; conventional Victorian fiancées and wives did not lightly use first names to the gentlemen of their choice.

For that matter, his friends in Springfield did not call him "Abe" either. He preferred to have them call him simply "Lincoln." He had a certain inner dignity that held off too great a degree of familiarity. It was a quality in him that many were to notice and some thought it was rooted in his essential goodness and integrity and his reserve of intellectual strength.

Mary was asked years later, after many great events had occurred, to give a full description of Mr. Lincoln and the result was a portrait which still remains one of the best and most understanding. In addition, after he became the center of her life and because of her great pride in him, she wrote much about him in her letters. She gave ample and indisputable evidence of what she thought of him later. It is perhaps legitimate to use hindsight here, taking her summing up of his qualities after years of intimate life with him as a key to what she instinctively recognized in the man who had courted her and won her love.

Furthermore, though this is the story of Abraham Lincoln and Mary Todd in the period of their courtship, one has a wish to know how these young personalities developed, to see them whole, to look into their future and reason back from subsequent events and statements about their incipient attitudes toward each other at this time. If this affords glimpses of what their marriage will be like, that will give one the satisfaction of those unregenerate individuals who peep at the end of a book to see how the story is going to turn out.

How did the tall, ungainly Mr. Lincoln look to Molly? His expressive face with its appealing combination of gentleness and strength had grown inexpressibly dear to her, but in an age which liked its masculine beauty smooth and conventional and did not appreciate ruggedness, it was considered anything but handsome. He was gaunt and homely in the eyes of Mary's sisters and, for that matter, in his own. The hardships, exposure, and unbalanced diet of his early years had made his skin sallow and wrinkled. As he once expressed it whimsically: "In my poor, lean, lank face nobody has ever seen that any cabbages were sprouting out." His appearance was not helped by the fact that he had neither the knowledge nor resources to dress himself to advantage. One suspects that the disproportionate length of arms and legs was often emphasized by sleeves and trousers that were too short.

To one who gave such careful thought to clothes as

Mary Todd, this unawareness must have had peculiar force. It was true that he had advanced a long way in taste since he had come to Springfield, had bought new clothes and lost some of his countrified look, but in New Salem a very few years before, he had presented anything but a romantic appearance. A friend there noted that "there was one half foot space between bottom of pants and top of socks." Another friend went into details: "His pants were made of *flax and tow*, cut tight at the ankle — *his knees were both out*. Was the toughest looking man I ever saw — poor boy, but welcomed to every body's house." The appealing magnetism of the young Lincoln won out even over these handicaps; the description concludes that he *"had nothing only plenty of friends."*

Any woman, especially one with Mary's motherly instinct, could see that he needed taking in hand with regard to dress. It may have hurt her pride a little that he did not resemble the current fashion plates as much as did the other gentlemen in the coterie, but she knew this was not a vital matter. The time would come when, as his wife, she would see that he had the proper clothes, when she would spend long hours making him fine shirts by hand in order that he might be as well dressed as others. It was also a matter of sentiment with her: she could not endure the thought of her husband's wearing shirts made by any hands but her own.

She was to learn that she would have to give him an all-over, searching look before he left the house to see that he had not forgotten anything essential, and to supply the umbrella or warm shawl the weather required.

Mary herself, when she had been married less than half a dozen years, said that Mr. Lincoln was "not pretty." But then something of her feeling for the quality of that rough-hewn face flashed out in her choice of adjective as she added with wifely pride and confidence: "Doesn't he look as if he would make a magnificent President?" It was written of her that "she was inordinately proud of her tall and ungainly husband. . . . If to other persons he seemed homely, to her he was the embodiment of noble manhood. . . ." If this was true after years of marriage, one is safe in assuming it was true with the romantic girl in the first glow of their engagement.

Lack of assurance in dress possibly contributed to his trouble in adjusting himself to Springfield society, though he was never to have too much awareness of clothes, and suits of the most impeccable stylishness soon assumed a rumpled and casual air when he put them on. The personality of the man dominated what he wore and one has difficulty imagining the tall, loose figure stiffened into the straight lines of a uniform or adjusted to the elaborateness of a colonial costume.

The girl who never failed to respond to longing or distress in the eyes of a child must surely have sensed his unsureness of himself at parties, his not knowing how to behave, his need for a woman's help, his wistfulness for the advantages he had missed in early life.

That this feeling of lack stayed with him is shown by an incident which occurred many years later. It was related by a fellow lawyer who traveled with Mr. Lincoln on the judicial circuit. One evening at Danville, Illinois, after the day's legal work was over, Mr. Lincoln disappeared. His friends and roommates (for they often slept many to a room at the crowded inns) were puzzled at his absence and searched for him. Without his interesting companionship and funny stories, the evening seemed very dull and they finally went to bed without him.

When the latch of the bedroom door was raised and Mr. Lincoln tiptoed in, one of his friends exclaimed: "Why Lincoln, where *have* you been?" "I was in hopes you fellers would be asleep," was the answer and then he explained he had been to a little country show, given chiefly for school children. He disappeared the next night too, for the show was still in town, and on his return described the features of the entertainment, which had included a magic lantern. His friend who related the story remarked that he had seen all these sights at school. "Yes," replied Lincoln, "I now have an advantage over you in, for the first time in my life, seeing these things which are of course common to those, who had, what I did not, a chance at an education when they were young."

He always kept that attitude of trying to acquire more knowledge, partly perhaps to catch up with what he had missed, partly because of the eager intellectual curiosity by which he continued to grow. Once, as President, at a White House reception, he held up the long line of people waiting to shake his hand while he explained to Judge David Davis, the very judge who had traveled with him on the judicial circuit, that he had just learned to spell the word "maintenance." In pleased and boyish fashion he spelled it out, syllable by syllable — surely unique behavior in a formally attired President greeting guests at a presidential reception.

By that time Lincoln had developed inner strength to the point where he dared to be his natural self under all circumstances. But that was a long way from the time when, as a young man, he was trying to adjust himself to Springfield society. In his earliest photograph, taken perhaps four years after he was married, one sees an expression of strain and uncertainty, and a somewhat pathetic look in the eyes. That may well have been due to the long, trying minutes of holding still which were required by the then new and wonderful daguerreotype process, but this is the nearest one can get to the face of the young man who courted Mary Todd and there may be here something resembling that wistful look that she had seen in her lover's face.

What quality of Mr. Lincoln's did Mary mention first when she in later life was asked to describe him? He was the "kindest man" in the world, she said, and the "most loving." She spoke of his great indulgence for those he loved, his praise for the good in them, his dislike of imposing his will or restraint upon them. The emotionally unstable girl may unconsciously have sensed that here was one who would pass her "imperfections lightly by," who would deal gently, understandingly, and paternally with her undisciplined and often headstrong spirit. He was in the future to call her his "child-wife" and excuse her faults as he would those of a child. And in the end she was to recognize and put it into writing that he had spoiled her with his indulgence.

But to Molly in love at the end of 1840, who perhaps felt

that since the death of her mother she had not been vitally important to anyone, it was doubtless sweet and gratifying to receive this gentle spoiling that was part of a paternal man's love for her. His uncritical attitude may have seemed a welcome relief after living with the various Todds, who were very outspoken about her failings. And to the affectionate and love-starved Lincoln it meant everything to have someone of his very own to pet and humor.

Her letters later are starred with mention of his "great tenderness" and "gentleness of character," just as their life together was filled with incidents which illustrated these qualities. One can safely say that she found them also in his lovemaking.

Molly and Mr. Lincoln could laugh and have fun together. He could playfully call her "Puss." They used the language of light imagining, of fanciful make-believe. He could be irresistibly whimsical and droll. When she sought for words to describe this dear playfulness, she spoke of his being "cheery, funny," "in high spirits," and "almost boyish in his mirth."

She was not the only one to observe and label this boyishness. A friend who knew him well thought that Lincoln had three characteristic moods. The first was a business mood when he gave strict attention to the matter in hand and what to do about it, grappled with the problem, and worked his way logically to its solution. The second was the melancholy mood, the "blues" already encountered in his letters to Miss Owens. Mary perhaps had not become fully acquainted with this failing of his yet, but she was shortly to learn about it in perhaps its worst manifestation, to come up against a crushing, all-out melancholia in the man she loved.

The third mood, continued Lincoln's friend, was a *"don't-care-whether-school-keeps-or-not"* one, in which he had the appealing recklessness of an irresponsible small boy. When in this humor, he would tease and play pranks. He carried this trait far into his later life and one finds an incident of it in the year when he was forty-seven and even being mentioned as a possible candidate for Vice-President. Traveling on the judicial circuit, he had stopped at an inn in Urbana where the landlord delighted to beat with great vigor upon a particularly loud and obnoxious dinner gong. Lincoln watched his chance to seize and hide this offending object. Then, while the landlord searched distractedly, the prankster sat awkwardly in a chair tilted up in the usual fashion, "looking amused, silly and guilty, as if he had done something ridiculous, funny and reprehensible."

Equally characteristic was his creeping into the dining room a little later and, while his friend held the doors fast against intruders, restoring the gong to its accustomed place. Then "he bounded up the stairs, two steps at a time. . . ."

Perhaps a certain boyishness is part of the fundamental simplicity which one so often finds in the truly great. At all events, a maternal woman delights in this quality in the man she loves.

As to "his mirth" which she spoke of, it was irresistible. A gentleman was to remark about Mr. Lincoln: "He was . . . wise, but O Lord wasn't he funny?" Doubtless in the gay assemblies of the coterie that fall Mary's ear had become especially attuned to hear that ringing, inimitable laugh which was to become so famous. He wrinkled his nose as he laughed and his body shook all over with merriment. Its forerunner was a twinkle in the gray eyes, a twinkle so infectious that years later his little son Tad was to start laughing uproariously as soon as he saw it. Mary may have learned in the months of courtship to watch eagerly for that fun light in Lincoln's eyes. Her gaiety gave quick response to it, though her sense of humor was a different and lesser thing. It is to be doubted whether her eyes ever twinkled with tolerant amusement in the way his did, though they could sparkle with mischief, flash blue fire in anger, or light up with joyousness.

Her humor was apt to concern itself with the individual or the present moment. In its maturity his was the great type of humor whose reverse side is a terrible, crushing pity for the sorrows of mankind. His ear was attuned to hear "the still, sad music of humanity." This man of torturing sensitivity could laugh, but he could also weep, and sometimes he laughed in order not to weep.

But this is looking ahead to the time when Lincoln entered history. To the engaged couple it was enough that they could laugh, be playful, use their imaginations, and have fun together.

One doubts whether the young girl had discovered at the end of 1840 all of Mr. Lincoln's characteristics. Marriage properly should contain a few surprises. She was to learn that he — to use her own words — "was a terribly firm man when he set his foot down," that no one, including herself, "could rule him after he had made up his mind." The outward sign that he had arrived at an immovable decision, she said, was that "he pressed or compressed his lips tightly, firmly, one against the other." One can see this firm closing of the lips in later photographs, but it is not so apparent in the earliest one. Young Mr. Lincoln is shortly to be seen in a frantic state of indecision, one that almost tore him apart. His firmness, like some of his other qualities, was to develop under the circumstances life would bring to him.

Certainly in the tender world of their new betrothal she had not discovered what she did discover later: that he could sometimes speak "crabbedly to men" (her own words) and could even boot an insolent rascal out of his office in righteous anger. He would at times in the future become impatient with her, but it would never get very far past his tenderness. She was to speak of him as being "so gentle and easy" and of his having "peaceful nerves." Again this is a glimpse of later development, for not long after this time of their engagement, he was to make a statement indicating he thought he had "defective nerves." They were anything but peaceful in the crisis that was about to overwhelm these two.

She was also to say that, with all his "deep feeling, he was *not* a demonstrative man, when he felt most deeply, he expressed the least." This calmness was to be a foil to her excitability, but this too was a self-control achieved later; he is soon, in this story, to give most immoderate expression to his suffering.

This couple had a broad and congenial meeting ground in their love of literature. She had grown up with the riches of her father's library; she had studied with the cultured Dr. Ward; she had so much stored-up literary treasure to share with him. In his future busy life she was to go through books in which they were interested and give him the gist of them.

Anyone who said the word "poetry" to either Mr. Lincoln or Mary was sure to meet with an immediate and responsive interest. It was an age that allowed itself to enjoy uncomplicated poetry in a natural way as something fine and beautiful. Most of the coterie were poetry conscious. Mr. Lincoln had a remarkable memory and Mary an excellent one; both knew many favorite poems by heart. One can imagine them repeating these verses to each other, each enjoying the feel and rhythm of the beloved lines anew in the other's responsive delight. Passages from Shakespeare were stored up like keepsakes in their minds and the repetition of them led into the subject of drama, which was also a mutual delight. Neither was ever to miss a play or show of any kind if it was possible to attend it, until that last fatal theater-going when they sat hand in hand gazing intently upon the lighted stage while an assassin crept up in the shadows behind them.

Burns was another favorite with both. That Lincoln felt a kinship for Robert Burns was natural; the Scots poet too in youth had known poverty, hard labor, and an aching desire for books and he expressed the sympathy for lowly people that Lincoln felt so strongly. It was part of his great democracy. Mary also was so devoted to Burns that in later life she made a reverent pilgrimage to his birthplace. As for the ideas in his poems, she was soon emphatically to demonstrate her own conviction that, in spite of snobbish expressions to the contrary being dinned in her ears, "a man's a man for a' that."

It meant much to this couple that they could enter the same poetic moods together, always a precious employment to young people in love. It was a congeniality that ran deep. He was working toward a literary style of his own, striving for the beauty of clarity, simplicity, and essential truth. He had a feeling for the incantation of words, for the enchantment of language. Each in writing was guided by a mental cadence that tested the rhythm and flow of the sentences. Hers was the femininely ornate, involved style of the Victorian age, with an excess of commas used like small frills; his was to attain a majestic simplicity that, like the Bible, belongs to no one era but is timeless.

Both attempted to write poetry, of course. Before long in this story certain rather too clever verses of Mary's composing will result in serious trouble for Mr. Lincoln and herself. They were personal and witty, as one would expect, but his poetic efforts tended toward somber and philosophic thoughts. When he visited the scene of his Indiana home about fifteen years after he left it, he tried to put his emotions into verse:

> My childhood-home I see again,
>   And gladden with the view;
> And still as mem'ries crowd my brain,
>   There's sadness in it too.

It was a very sad revisiting, for his mother and only sister lay buried there, and the many verses are melancholy. Lincoln's "Bear Hunt" makes much more lively reading;

it is a narrative by a master storyteller. In the following stanza one gets a picture of him as a young boy in Indiana awakened from sleep in the cabin at night and cringing at the terrifying sounds of the dark and savage world outside.

> When first my father settled here,
>   'Twas then the frontier line:
> The panther's scream, filled night with fear
>   And bears preyed on the swine.

It is not surprising to learn that these two poetry-loving people would one day have a son who, as a child, wrote verses.

Two people cannot share literary interests without each discovering the intellectual caliber of the other. Mary plainly liked brainy people. She said herself she preferred a man of mind. She had found him. In their married life it was a subject on which she loved to dwell. Referring to the Lincoln-Douglas debates, she said with shining eyes that Mr. Lincoln was an intellectual giant and in this regard towered above Douglas as much as he did physically, that Douglas was " a very little, *little* giant" beside her husband. Again mentioning these two, she added that Mr. Lincoln's heart "is as large as his arms are long," thus making her wifely boasting include the two fundamental qualities of his personality. Her confidence in his talents was to rise above momentary disappointments and be a prop to his not too hopeful spirit; she was to look forward triumphantly to his future greatness and when that greatness was finally achieved, no one was to speak of it in more glowing and superlative terms than herself. She wrote after his death that some in his own generation "were only beginning to comprehend the nature and nobility of the great, good man, who had accomplished his work, and before *his Judge*, it was pronounced complete."

She sensed that he reached the full measure of his statesmanship by a process of growth. Describing his struggle in the wartime Presidency, she said: "When we first went to Washington many persons thought that Mr. Lincoln was weak, but he rose grandly with the circumstances of the case, and men soon learned that he was above them all. I never saw a man's mind develop itself so finely."

One wonders whether the engaged couple touched upon the subject of religion. It was probably a grief to Mary's married life that Mr. Lincoln never joined a church, though he attended church with her and paid rent on their family pew. He could not accept some of the narrow orthodoxy that prevailed a century ago and his joining would have implied an acceptance that was not true. He could not act a falsehood. Mary said of him justly that he "was *truth itself*."

When asked about his church membership, she answered simply: "He was a religious man always. . . ." She quoted what Lincoln had often said to her when her spirit blazed in hot defiance of those who schemed against him: "Do good to those who hate you and turn their ill will to friendship." He believed, as he said, in loving God and one's neighbor, and lived by this belief.

It was perhaps her recognition of a certain mystic quality of his faith that she had in mind when she made that most understanding statement about him: He "had a kind of poetry in his nature."

Mary Todd saw in Mr. Lincoln a man who needed her and her care and love. It is fulfillment to a woman to give these things. She saw a man who was congenial, with whom she enjoyed herself, a man who had a powerful intellect combined with tenderness, one in whose future she could have supreme confidence. But in the multitude of things she said and wrote about him, expressions of love for him predominate. He was her "darling," her "beloved," her "idolized," her "dearly loved one." She said of herself and her children: ". . . we never felt, notwithstanding our *great* love for him . . . that we could love him sufficiently." Unlike Lincoln she was and remained demonstrative and gave full outlet to her emotions. As that understanding and beloved friend and physician, Dr. Anson G. Henry, said: ". . . she loved him as women of her nervous sanguine temperament, only can love. . . ."

In her bright but ill-balanced nature there was not the promise of building up to greatness as in his but the menace of breakdown under strain. She would not be able to rise to meet the circumstances of her case; the shadow of her downward trend would fall poignantly upon him as he "rose grandly" to meet his. But her devotion to him and her faith in him would never waver. The sum of her qualities did not add up to greatness, but she had a great love.

CHAPTER 9

Without Her "No Variety"

WHAT did Mr. Lincoln see in Molly, his fiancée at the end of 1840? What did he learn about her as he sat listening to her sparkling chatter in the spellbound fashion described by Mrs. Edwards? One doubts very much whether the role of listener was always his, as Mrs. Edwards thought. Mary had her own role as listener to play in the future. Years later when, as First Lady, she was away from Washington on a trip, she explained her anxiety to get back to her husband, saying "with much feeling" that he was lonely when she was away and needed her to laugh at his jokes and funmaking at table. Then she added with that wifely pride that was always to be in evidence that no matter how hard he worked during the day or how tired he was, he was always lively, sociable, and agreeable. So perhaps he managed, when Mrs. Edwards was not present, to contribute something to their conversations.

The topics they chose to talk about are necessarily a matter of guesswork, but it is known that certain experiences and memories were in the minds of both. In their conversations Lincoln doubtless learned much of the background of this girl, with all that that background implied in her make-up and her views. She would naturally tell him something of her girlhood in Kentucky, especially as they had that state in common as a birthplace. He may have felt keenly the contrast between the log cabin which witnessed the grim birth of a man child to his pioneer mother, a "granny woman" perhaps assisting, and the stately Southern home into which she came, to be ministered to by a whole staff of Negro slaves and surrounded by parents and relatives of assured prominence.

A favorite topic with Mary was Mammy Sally, who had "raised" her, a jewel of a black mammy whose quaint words and accent came to life on the girl's lips. Mary's gift for drama and mimicry was irresistible; she could hold a roomful of people spellbound, as well as a bashful suitor. As her brother-in-law Ninian once remarked, while he chuckled over her ludicrous imitations: "Mary could make a bishop forget his prayers."

There were so many rich stories to tell about Mammy. She had been determined to raise Mary and her brothers and sisters right; she gave them instruction of a special flavor and dramatic power. She impressed upon them the ominous fact that jay birds went to hell every Friday night to tell the "debil" all the bad things they had done during the week. Mr. Jay would twitter in "ole man Satan's ears" such items as: "Mary hid Mammy's slippers when po' old Mammy was tryin' to res' her foots in the garden after lopin' 'roun' all day after bad chil'en."

"Ole man Satan" was a formidable individual who, according to Mammy Sally, had horns and a pea-green tail. Little Mary had liked to argue about this, saying the tail would naturally be black, not green, but Mammy would put that heresy down with a "No, chile, you must not demoralize the holy word which I heared out'en the preacher's own mouth, right at your pa's dinner table."

The jay birds sometimes had a heavy lot of iniquities to report. Mary was a little prankster and Mammy occasionally got an annoying surprise, such as finding salt instead of sugar in her coffee. Such a surprise was apt to be followed by an emphatic remark about that "limb of Satan." In the end little Mary was likely to make amends by the gift of a red and yellow bandanna handkerchief or something equally desirable.

In this playful prankishness Mary's sense of humor met Mr. Lincoln's. Any friend who knew the engaged couple intimately might well have predicted that if there were children of this marriage, they would be full of mischief, a prediction that was to be abundantly fulfilled.

For all her love of Mammy Sally, Cheney the cook, and old Nelson, who, clad in a blue swallowtail coat with big brass buttons, ceremoniously served mint juleps to her father's visitors, Mary had seen the dark and cruel side of slavery. Floggings at that black-locust whipping post in the center of Lexington were public and accompanied by heart-rending screams. Slave traders drove their chained gangs of slaves, manacled two abreast, past the front door of the Todd home on Main Street. Revolting cases of cruelty had occurred in Lexington which little Mary, with white face, talked about in shocked whispers.

She was a tenderhearted girl. Pain and injustice to others hurt her and aroused her indignation, just as they did that of Mr. Lincoln. If the engaged couple talked of slavery's cruelties, they felt alike about it. Both at that time believed in the abolition of slavery by gradual emancipation with compensation to slave owners. In the future, as slavery became a burning issue in the country, their views about it were to undergo change and expand, but always they would move forward in the same direction and be united in the way they looked at the subject.

A part of the belated but liberal education which Lincoln was so rapidly absorbing in Springfield was enlightenment as to the Southern views on slavery. Through Mary he came to know how a Southern family loved its house servants, who tyrannized in paradoxical fashion over a home that was only a few steps from a slave pen and not far from the auction block and whipping post on Lexington's square. He doubtless found out much too in his discussions with Joshua Speed, who came from a plantation in Kentucky; in fact, an impressive number of the people in the social circle at Springfield had a Southern background. This knowledge of the Southern viewpoint was to be useful to Lincoln later; when civil war came, he would know how to keep a border state like Kentucky in the Union.

In believing in gradual emancipation, Mary was following the lead of her adored idol, the great Whig chieftain, Henry Clay, who lived in her home town, Lexington. He was a topic on which she and Mr. Lincoln undoubtedly talked glowingly, for, by what the lovers doubtless considered a beautiful arrangement of Providence, Henry Clay was also Mr. Lincoln's "beau-ideal" of a statesman.

Mr. Lincoln had worshiped Henry Clay and his ideals at a distance, but Mary had known and loved him as her father's friend. She could tell her fiancé how Mr. Clay looked when he visited in her home in Lexington, could describe the tall, slender figure, the high forehead and gray eyes, the engaging voice, and the grace with which he took snuff or perchance accepted a mint julep from old Nelson. In the years of Lincoln's Presidency there would be those who compared his tall, spare figure to that of Clay and the romantic girl may well have thought of such a welcome resemblance. She, as a young girl, had been completely captivated by Mr. Clay's magnetism, and thereby hangs a story which one hopes she told Mr. Lincoln, for he would have enjoyed it.

At the age of thirteen she had one day mounted a just-acquired white pony and ridden out to Mr. Clay's to show him her proud new possession. A pretty word picture has been drawn of this little girl, with her vivid rosy face and flying light brown curls framed in a sunbonnet, racing along the road to Ashland, Mr. Clay's home. There she was kindly invited to dinner and had the bliss of listening to much talk of politics between Mr. Clay and several visiting gentlemen of prominence. Such a topic with such a listening-in constituted one of her greatest delights when important politicians came to her father's house to dine. It was well for their congeniality that she had grown up in an atmosphere of Whig politics, the party to which Mr. Lincoln was so devoted.

They could talk about this absorbing subject of politics without the intrusion of that cramping idea that females should not strain their feeble mentalities with weighty questions fit only for masculine intellects. Mr. Lincoln in regard to this notion, as in so many others, seemed untouched by the stilted thought patterns of his age. This may have been one of the reasons why Mary, impatient of restraint, was drawn to him. Even if she did wish to be thought appealingly feminine, no girl of the Victorian age could have enjoyed being thought too dumb to grapple with weighty subjects about which all the while she was sure she knew just as much as the gentlemen themselves and probably had more resourceful ideas.

In the future ahead of them he was to keep her in touch with each political move he made, tell her about his speeches, and talk things over with her, getting her quick reactions. She would bolster his morale in his self-doubting moments. It was said of him that "his ambition was a little engine that knew no rest." Her little engine of ambition was to run side by side with his.

He would respect her shrewdness, her "sagacity," to use his own word, and profit by it, but he was also to recognize that she was "too suspicious" and "disposed to magnify trifles." And she would answer to the charge that she was suspicious that he was too confiding, "too honest for this world," that he "should have been born a saint." All of which was wholesome give and take of discussion and apt to lead to a balanced consideration of the subject in hand. She thought he "had not much knowledge of men." Her suspicions, growing out of her instinct to protect him from his own goodness, were meant to safeguard him.

One wonders whether Molly and Mr. Lincoln touched upon a certain dark topic, an event of deep pain and lasting scar which both had experienced in childhood. There was a place in the mind of each, perhaps walled off from too casual entrance, which was filled with the memory of the same tragedy. Lincoln had lost his mother when he was nine, Mary when she was going on seven. He had seen still and sunken in death the face to which he, up to that time, had looked as the center of his child life, had witnessed the lowering of the homemade coffin without religious ceremony into a lonely grave in the backwoods. Ever after, death was to cast him into gloom far more than normal; ever after, the sight of a loved dead face was to throw Mary almost into convulsions. He was to find that the poem which asked, "Oh, why should the spirit of mortal be proud?" expressed the melancholy questioning that arose from such overpowering pain and grief. The sadness that entered the eyes of that young boy in the wilderness was to reappear in the eyes of the grown man who was subject to terrible spells of melancholia. Death laid another scar on his sensitive spirit when he was nineteen; his only sister died in a peculiarly cruel way, in the primitive, unattended childbirth of the frontier.

Death was always terrible to Mr. Lincoln. Even in the White House, strong and self-controlled as he had become by the time he entered it, he was to weep man tears over the deaths of certain dear friends killed in the war, was to break down over the mere mention of their names and be unable to speak. His love for his friends ran deep, but perhaps his reaction to the tragedy of death, especially of the young, involved something of the vast pity for mankind with which he was obsessed.

Death had struck frequently in the hard frontier conditions under which he had grown up. The helplessness, grief, and questioning of bereaved people were almost more than he could bear. He had been deeply depressed over the case of a young woman who had been a member of the friendly family with whom he boarded for a while in New Salem. She had been engaged to a friend of his whom he called "Mack" (John McNamar) and she died of a fever while her fiancé was far away. He had returned shortly after her death expecting to be married to her. In his sorrow John McNamar, as he told himself later, went to the lonely grave of the girl he had loved and carved the initials A.R. on a headboard, for the name of the girl was Ann Rutledge. Lincoln had grieved deeply, as did the whole community, over the pity and sadness of this death.

He never mentioned this incident to Mary. Nor is it known how much he told her about his mother at the time they became engaged, but it is certain that ultimately he painted for her a loving picture of the mother he had lost. Mary later wrote: "He had often described to me, his noble mother" and how she had told him stories from the Bible and prayed that he would "become a pious boy & man." For Lincoln's mother and his loved stepmother both Mary had great tenderness. A loving letter she wrote Sarah Lincoln, his stepmother, exists today, saying: "If I can ever be of any service to you in *any respect* I am entirely at your service." It is a letter appropriately signed "Affectionately yours."

For all her vitality and buoyancy Mary was occasionally ill. By his own statement Mr. Lincoln learned early in their acquaintance that she was subject to devastating headaches, the kind that laid her low in an agony of pain that made any noise or even a jarring step on the floor pure torture. Nowadays these are called migraine headaches and they often go with just the type of personality Mary Todd had.

A doctor at the Mayo Clinic is said to have told his classes of young men getting ready to go into medical practice, where a good wife would be a most valuable asset: "I say to you, go and find yourself a fine migraine patient and marry her!" He meant that these headaches go with a definite personality type which the doctor described as follows: "When she isn't sick, she's likely to be a lot of fun and far more keen and interested than the average woman." Lincoln's initial interest in Mary Todd perhaps commenced with his finding her just that: "a lot of fun" and "keen and interested."

In spite of being in love with Mary, Lincoln (whose letters of this time show that he had learned a lot about human nature in the rough school of his upbringing) probably had some inkling of her weaknesses: her impulsiveness which was often imprudence, her quickness to fly into anger or panic and to be irresponsible in both, her lack of restraint in using her tongue. He really liked the sauciness of that tongue; it was, as he said later with a chuckle, a Todd trait, it ran in the family. In the future he was to joke, as others did, about the temper and spunkiness of the Todds and one gathers that Mary and her relatives did not mind this too much but rather enjoyed the distinction.

Once in later years when Mr. Lincoln was traveling on the circuit with various other lawyers, including Mary's cousin John Todd Stuart, an affable landlady at the inn where they were stopping greeted them thus: "Stuart, how fine and peart you do look!, but Lincoln, whatever have you been a doing? you do look powerful weak." Mr. Lincoln answered with a droll face: "Nothing out of common, Ma'am, but did you ever see Stuart's wife? or did you ever see mine? I just tell you whoever married into the 'Todd' family gets the worst of it."

In the merriment which followed, the other lawyers joined in the banter and began naming over the various ones in Springfield who had married Todds. They found to their glee that all except portly William Wallace, husband of Mary's sister Frances, were thin enough to prove the point. One can almost hear Mr. Lincoln's booming laugh at this winning of his case.

One finds him later teasing his wife to "get a rise" out of her, to enjoy a tall, tolerant man's amusement at the retorts of a spirited little woman.

At those times when she was under strain and not well and her tongue lashing went to extremes he would say quietly: "It does her lots of good and it doesn't hurt me a bit." He knew he could always count on her being sorry when she was herself again. He was to meet her emotional immaturity paternally. "Will you be a *good girl* in all things," he was to write her later, if he would consent to let her have her own way in a certain matter.

Lincoln recognized that he had to choose his wife from among imperfect human beings, that being the only kind available, and that what he was offering her was an imperfect human. In his own mind his shortcomings were printed in capital letters and hers in tiny type.

The sentimental writing of the time laid stress on lovers who were wedded and "lived happily ever after" in a rather impossible state of bliss as stiff and artificial as the contemporary prints which have the title "Married." In any age a man of common sense knows that the matrimonial menu cannot consist of sweets alone. There should be the appetizer of physical attraction, the bread and meat of mutual endeavor in building up a life together, the tart salad of differences (which may have considerable pepper and vinegar without spoiling the flavor), the dessert of deep-rooted companionship, and the joy of parental pride. All these things the Lincoln marriage was to have in full measure.

What Mr. Lincoln saw in Mary was a young woman he found desirable, the one he wanted for his wife. By her own statement, he told her, both before and after marriage, she was the only one he ever really loved. What did a difficult temperament amount to against the force of this? Her aristocratic background did not fit her for the wife of a poor man who was in debt, but on the other hand it did fit her to teach him social usages that had been no part of his growing up. She would one day make a gracious and cultured hostess for him when his political ambitions materialized. Because she was at one with him in his ambition he would always be eager to tell her of his triumphs, small or great, to double his pleasure in them by her joy. When the message came that he had been nominated and when the dispatch came that he had been elected President, he hurried away from excited, rejoicing friends to tell "a little woman" at home the news.

She was to furnish the color of his life, for by nature his thoughts ran to grays and black and white. He was to give this away in what he wrote her later when she had gone on a visit in 1848 and he missed her. He said that when she had been with him (he was then in Washington in Congress), she had taken his time away from his business, but now that she had gone and he had "nothing but business — no variety" it had grown "exceedingly tasteless" to him. Her response to living was vibrant, his philosophic.

They felt alike in ways of friendship; it constituted one of life's great values to each. They gave deep affection to their friends and grieved at parting from them. When Mercy left Springfield, Molly wrote her forlornly: "To me it has ever appeared that those whose presence was the sunlight of my heart have departed — separated — far and wide, to meet when?" Joshua Speed was to leave Springfield and Lincoln was to write him in strangely similar mood: "How miserably things seem to be arranged in this world. If we have no friends, we have no pleasure; and if we have them, we are sure to lose them, and be doubly pained by the loss." In the future these two, giving thus richly of friendliness, would know how, as a couple, to be good neighbors in Springfield.

It foretold a supreme joy of their future marriage that both Mary and Mr. Lincoln had a signal love for children. He had doubtless seen the softness in her eyes as she looked down at a child or tenderly lifted a baby in her arms; she the delight in his face as he tossed a little boy high in the air, as he often tossed the Butler children at the home where he was boarding.

Lincoln himself said that the first attraction that led to falling in love began with a man's liking the girl's personal appearance and manner. He liked Molly's prettiness, her dainty dress, her quick gestures of small white hands, her femininity. He was to be proud of his wife's looks; one can get a glimpse of this by borrowing an incident from their married life in Springfield. He had come home from his office to find her arrayed in a new dress she had made herself, a white silk with little bunches of blue flowers scattered over it. She loved to make herself pretty for him and he responded with a shining in his eyes and a smiling remark about her "fine feathers." Then he added while she bridled with delight: "Those posies on your dress are the color of your eyes."

Molly was a born flirt. She could use to perfection the Victorian brand of coquetry of tossed head, of toying fan, and of sprightly retort without for a minute compromising her helplessness, her "weak woman's" need for masculine protection. Such coquetry is apt to seem outmoded and a bit silly now, but one may be sure it was just what the Victorian man wanted or the Victorian girls would not have employed it. Each generation has its own methods to attract; it is the attraction between man and maid that remains perennially the same.

Mr. Lincoln liked Mary's coquetry, though there is reason to believe that shortly after they became engaged there was an example of it he did not like, and this led to trouble. He would play up to her coquettishness in the future. One catches the flavor of this playfulness in one of his letters to her after their marriage when he wrote whimsically: "I am afraid you will get so well, and fat, and young, as to be wanting to marry again."

He was always in their married life to want her with him. "I hate to stay in this old room by myself," he wrote her when she was away. He was to seek her out in those all too few moments of relaxation which were his in the White House. Their friends were to notice the light in his eyes as he gazed at her and one was to describe it as "the *pleasing look of Abraham Lincoln* — for *her whom he so loved*."

What Mr. Lincoln saw in Mary Todd, to whom he was engaged at the end of the year 1840, is summed up in a few words of his more than twenty years later. A friend chatting with them in the great East Room of the White House noticed how the President's eyes followed his wife. Suddenly realizing that he was caught in the act, Mr. Lincoln laughed pleasantly and said: "My wife is as handsome as when she was a girl, and I, a poor nobody then, fell in love with her.

"And what is more," he continued, "I have never fallen out."

CHAPTER **10**

"That Fatal First of Jany."

ON Friday, New Year's Day 1841, an event occurred which seared Lincoln's very soul. At the Edwards home that night there were tears on Mary's pillow. Rumors began to fly from tongue to tongue in the coterie. Mr. Lincoln's friends in the legislature could notice that his face was tragic in its sadness. He did not attend the session on Monday though he was present each day for the rest of the week. On the Friday following New Year's someone evidently twitted him on that sore point, the jumping-out-of-the-window episode of the month before. Mr. Lincoln answered with uncharacteristic testiness that "as to jumping, he should jump when he pleased and no one should hinder him." The tall lawyer was not himself at all; he was sunk in melancholia, he looked terrible and as if he were "coming down" with an illness, which indeed he was.

He managed to attend the legislature up to January 13, then he was confined to his room and word went to his loved friend and physician, Dr. Henry, to come and take charge of the case. A vivid description of the way he looked when he reappeared in public is given in a letter of the invaluable Mr. Conkling to Mercy: "Poor L! how are the mighty fallen! He was confined about a week, but though he now appears again he is reduced and emaciated in appearance and seems scarcely to possess strength enough to speak above a whisper." Mr. Conkling continued: "His case at present is truly deplorable but what prospect there may be for ultimate relief I cannot pretend to say. I doubt not but he can declare 'That loving is a painful thrill, And not to love more painful still' but would not like to intimate that he has experienced 'That surely 'tis the worst of pain To love and not be loved again.' " The news was out; the engagement between Mary and Abraham had been broken.

About the only help Mr. Lincoln could get in his agony of spirit came from the kind and understanding Dr. Henry. And at this time there was danger that he would leave Springfield, depriving his patient of that one comfort. On January 20 the lawyer wrote his partner John Todd Stuart asking that the physician be given the Springfield postmastership as an inducement for staying: "You know I desired Dr. Henry to have that place when you left; I now desire it more than ever. I have, within the last few days, been making a most discreditable exhibition of myself in the way of hypochondriaism and thereby got an impression that Dr. Henry is necessary to my existence. Unless he gets that place he leaves Springfield." Emphasizing that his heart was "verry much set" upon the appointment, Lincoln apologized for not writing a longer letter as he had not "sufficient composure" to do so.

Hypochondria was an ailment much talked of at this time. Its chief characteristic was a severe and distorting depression of mind and the word also carried the connotation of a morbid anxiety as to one's own health. Psychiatrists now get many patients who would have been pronounced hypochondriacs in the middle eighteen-hundreds.

Three days later the junior partner wrote to Mr. Stuart again, giving a striking description of his "blues." Mr. Lincoln had entered upon a strange and terrible psychological experience. Certain letters of his in the months ahead were to contain a remarkable unbosoming of inmost feelings. The emotional climate of the time was different from that of today; it was the style for people to analyze and express their sensations with a freedom from which one now shies away. Mr. Lincoln certainly had no reserve or inhibition when he wrote: "I am now the most miserable man living. If what I feel were equally distributed to the whole human family, there would not be one cheerful face on the earth. Whether I shall ever be any better I can not tell; I awfully forebode I shall not. To remain as I am is impossible; I must die or be better, it appears to me."

One can imagine the reaction of Mr. Stuart, who had left the law office in charge of his junior partner, as he read on: "The matter you speak of on my account, you may attend to as you say, unless you shall hear of my condition forbidding it. I say this, because I fear I shall be unable to attend to any bussiness here. . . ." Lincoln ended the letter because he could "write no more."

Various letters defining the situation went traveling back and forth. Mercy's sister-in-law, Mrs. Lawrason Levering, wrote to her "particulars about Abraham, Joshua, and Jacob. . . ." Mercy made answering comment in a letter to her lover: "Poor A—— I fear his is a blighted heart! perhaps if he was as persevering as Mr. W. he might be successful." Mr. W. was, of course, Mr. Webb, who was assiduously courting Mary himself and probably took delight in this sudden and mysterious break between her and Abraham.

"Jacob Faithful" replied to Mercy on March 7 giving a not too sympathetic account of Mr. Lincoln to date: "And L., poor hapless simple swain who loved most true but was not loved again — I suppose he will now endeavor to drown his cares among the intricacies and perplexities of the law." The next sentence suggests that Lincoln in social gatherings had been gratified (as is humanity in general) by a hearty response to one of his witticisms or stories: "No more will the merry peal of laughter ascend *high in the air*, to greet his listening and delighted ears. . . . alas! I fear his shrine will now be deserted and that he will withdraw himself from the society of us inferior mortals." Mr. Conkling was right; Mr. Lincoln was attending strictly to his own affairs and was not seen at the Edwards home and the gay assemblies of the coterie.

There were no private matters in a small prairie town in the eighteen-forties — or, as far as that goes, in a small town today. People were talking at a great rate about Mr. Lincoln's extraordinary state of depression. Some used the word "crazy" as applied to him. A slangy gentleman wrote John J. Hardin, on January 22: "We have been very much distressed, on Mr. Lincoln's account; hearing that he had two Cat fits and a Duck fit since we left."

Gossiping tongues were clicking excitedly, turning the choice morsel of the shattered love affair over and over again, elaborating on it, supplying out of imagination added details to make a good story. The engagement was broken. Why? Mr. Conkling thought Molly had jilted Mr. Lincoln; the gossips figured it out differently. Could Mr. Lincoln have fallen in love with another girl? There was that lovely Matilda Edwards who was visiting at the Edwards home; that must be it; Mr. Lincoln must have fallen in love with Matilda and jilted Miss Todd!

Such a satisfactory and delicious explanation went around, increasing in details, until it was a well-filled-out story. It is presented full blown in a letter written by a chatty young lady to a friend in Kentucky on January 27. One learns first that Mary is keeping her chin up: "Miss Todd is flourishing largely. She has a great many Beaus." Evidently the news of the Lincoln-Todd romance had penetrated into Kentucky, as the letter continues: "You ask me how she and Mr. Lincoln are getting along. Poor fellow, he is in a rather bad way. Just at present though he is on the mend now as he was out on Monday for the first time for a month dying with love they say." The week of illness had increased to a month, but that is a slow rate of growth for gossip. "Dying with love" was a popular theme with the sentimentalists of the time. "The Doctors say he came within an inch of being a perfect lunatic for life. He was perfectly crazy for some time, not able to attend to his business at all. They say he don't look like the same person."

Then comes the story: "It seems he had addressed Mary Todd and she accepted him and they had been engaged some time when a Miss Edwards of Alton came here, and he fell desperately in love with her and found he was not so much attached to Mary as he thought. He says if he had it in his power he would not have one feature of her face altered, he thinks she is so perfect (that is, Miss E.) He and Mr. Speed have spent the most of their time at Edwards this winter and Lincoln could never bear to leave Miss Edward's side in company. Some of his friends thought he was acting very wrong and very imprudently and told him so and he went crazy on the strength of it so the story goes and that is all I know. . . ." It can be determined later from a precious recently found letter written by Matilda herself whether what the writer "knew" about this falling in love was true.

These are the scattered references to the break in the engagement which were written down at the time. In an event such as this very few people know exactly what happened, perhaps only the two lovers themselves. It is a difficult task over a century later to turn detective and hunt out clues and scraps of evidence, to sift out the false from the true and reconstruct the emotional crisis that occurred on what Lincoln himself called "that fatal first of Jany. '41."

The most desirable account of an event is that written down at the time. Many years later, after Lincoln had become a great President and a martyr, questions were asked about this interruption in his love affair and the answers were jotted down. Ninian and Elizabeth Edwards were interviewed in their old age. Joshua Speed, portly and bearded, was asked to tell what he had known about it when he was a slender, romantic-faced young man. The information thus obtained is as likely to have undergone change as the appearance of the narrators; recollections are affected by the dimming of the years between, by the tricks that human memory plays upon itself, and by strong personal slants. These recollections come secondhand, through another mind and imagination, which always constitutes a hazard. From this mass of material certain explanations emerge which are consistent and fit into and are substantiated by the known facts.

In Lincoln's letters to Miss Owens there is indisputable evidence of his feeling that he had no right to marry because he had so little to offer a wife. Now appears a factor that affected that sensitive feeling like a dentist's instrument striking an exposed nerve. This was the opposition of Mary's family to the marriage. Mrs. Edwards stated definitely that she and her husband at first encouraged the friendship between Mary and Mr. Lincoln, then changed their minds and told them they should not marry.

In saying this, Mrs. Edwards gave as the reason for the opposition that the two were so different in their natures and rearing that they could not be happy together. It is true that Mary and Mr. Lincoln were complete opposites in a great many of their traits, but Mrs. Edwards was not exactly the one to understand the congeniality between them. The difference in the natures of the two was not the whole basis of Mrs. Edwards's objection. By the time she was asked for her account of the broken engagement, many events had occurred and many changes had come.

It would have been very embarrassing for her to admit, after Lincoln had reached the highest position in the land, that she had once opposed his marrying her sister on the ground that he was poor and had no prospects. Later her niece was more frank; she said plainly that the family regarded his future as "nebulous" and that it was also a matter of Lincoln's being "on a different social plane," of his having "no culture," of his being "ignorant of social forms and customs." Ninian, son of Governor Edwards, and Elizabeth, daughter of the Lexington Todds, looked down on Mr. Lincoln as a matter of class distinction. It was said of Ninian by one who knew him well that he "was naturally and constitutionally an aristocrat, and he hated democracy . . . as the devil is said to hate holy water." In general, the clan of Mary's relatives felt that in marrying Mr. Lincoln she would be marrying beneath her, a point of view which was handed down in the family to some extent in succeeding generations. In addition to the question of social inequality the clan for the most part held fundamental opinions which differed from those of Mr. Lincoln, their social and political philosophy clashed with his, they considered him a radical.

It is difficult to put one's finger upon the exact time when the Edwardses decided to reverse themselves and oppose the marriage. This disapproval may have developed and become evident gradually and may have been precipitated into active opposition by some special event. One knows from a letter of Mr. Conkling's that in October of 1840 Mary "did not appear as merry and joyous as usual," and from her own letter in December that she was losing weight and writing suggestively of "the *crime* of *matrimony*."

Albert Edwards, the son of the Ninian Edwardses, made some statements that prove helpful on this point. His testimony too comes long delayed and secondhand. He said that up to the time of the courtship his father and mother had made Lincoln welcome and encouraged his visits, but when his mother saw Mr. Lincoln was becoming serious, she treated him coldly and invitations to call "were not pressed." This, however, he added, did not have the effect intended. Albert Edwards said positively that during 1841 and 1842 his mother did what she could to break up the match. He thought that the opposition of his parents greatly influenced the breaking of the engagement.

Mrs. Edwards's remarks when she was being questioned about the love affair vibrate with disapproval and misunderstanding of Mr. Lincoln: he "was a cold man — had no affection — was not social." She admitted what the whole nation was saying by that time, that "he was a great man — a good man & an honest one," but he was, she said, "a little ungrateful," and "loved nothing." Ninian agreed that this "mighty Rough man" was not "warm hearted." It was only human nature that Mr. Edwards thought that any man who differed from him as radically as Lincoln did lacked mental capacity, or, to use Ninian's own words, was "not capable." Others in the family felt the same way; as one of them said later: "When he was nominated it seemed impossible that this should ever be," he was not "fitted for the position."

In setting forth the opposition of his parents to having Mr. Lincoln as a brother-in-law, Albert Edwards threw the emphasis on his mother's part. He believed that for years Mary resented the tactics which her sister Elizabeth had used "to discourage the engagement."

As mistress of the house where Mary was living, Mrs. Edwards could have had ample opportunity to make her disapproval evident to the sensitive young lawyer who socially was already suffering from an inferiority complex. One can easily imagine the cold and distinct greeting, the ignoring of his presence, the stony face following one of his humorous remarks. Any woman of the Todd family was apt to be good at showing her displeasure. Perhaps Mr. Lincoln, who was self-doubting at best, had been made uncomfortable for some time before the actual break in the engagement occurred.

One would give much to know what Ninian wrote Mary's father in answer to that letter inquiring as to the qualifications of Mr. Lincoln as suitor to Mary. Ninian at least knew Lincoln in the man's world of politics and business where he commanded respect, Mrs. Edwards only in the social setting where to her eyes he appeared to very poor advantage.

Apparently an incident involving a misunderstanding between the lovers preceded the actual breaking off of the engagement, an episode in which Mary hurt Mr. Lincoln's feelings by flirting ostentatiously with one of her other beaux. Later a niece of Mrs. Edwards and Mary, to whom the family account was handed down, dramatized this event: Mr. Lincoln, in modern phrase, forgot his date with Mary. He was to take her to a party, but, going into one of his characteristic periods of abstraction (in which he supposedly was meditating on all the reasons why it would not be fair to any girl for a man in his circumstances to marry her), he did not remember his appointment until after the hour had passed. Hurrying to the Edwards home, he found Mary had already gone to the party. When he followed her there, she, ignoring his presence, paid him back in true feminine fashion by an ostentatious flirtation with Mr. Douglas. Lincoln, deeply hurt, left the house without speaking with her. So runs the story and at least this dramatization is in character and it will be seen that Mary had a guilty conscience by a remark she made later.

With the background of the family disapproval of him, all the items which he had so carefully written out to Miss Owens as to the sad fate of any woman who would be "block-head" enough to marry him would naturally come flocking back to his mind. Mary had apparently done something to wound him and make him jealous; her family looked down on him and did not want to add him to the circle. Lincoln was deeply hurt. Ninian had been his friend; now he had joined his wife in advising against Lincoln's marrying into the family. They did not think he could support Mary in the manner to which she was accustomed and of course they were right; he could not. The girl herself was immature and ruled by her feelings; he must not take advantage of her or go against the judgment of those who were her natural protectors.

There was one ironic feature connected with the family opposition. If the Todd-Edwards clan did not want Lincoln as an in-law, in one sense he did not want them either. He was a man who believed in the people and in democracy. Politically he wanted the support of the common man. He foresaw that if he married into the aristocracy, he would have to defend himself against the accusation of sharing their views. That was just what happened to him in the end; less than five months after he was married he was, as he wrote from Springfield in some disgust, "put down here as the candidate of pride, wealth, and arristocratic family distinction." That, he said, would astonish, if not amuse, those who twelve years before "knew me a strange, friendless, uneducated, penniless boy, working on a flat boat — at ten dollars per month. . . ." His words point up the opposite points of view that were basic in the family opposition to the marriage.

According to Joshua Speed's account told about a quarter of a century later, Lincoln decided to write Mary a letter asking to be released from the engagement. One guesses that Joshua had been something of a guide to him in social usages and matters of taste as well as the close friend to whom he confided his inmost thoughts. An added element of Lincoln's great depression in early 1841 was the fact that Joshua was leaving Springfield. He sold his store on that same "fatal first" of January, a calamitous day for Lincoln's emotions in every respect, and he was to leave early in that year. They had shared the big room over that same store for four years. They had talked over the personal problems and matters that perplex young men. They had discussed religion and the institution of marriage and had raised skeptical questions about both, a skepticism that seems to have been shared by others in their group. At least, "Is the Married Life More Happy Than the Single" was the subject of an address (and doubtless much lively discussion) at a meeting of the Young Men's Lyceum. Lincoln felt bereft at Joshua's leaving.

He showed Joshua the letter he had written Mary asking to be released from the engagement. Joshua advised him not to send a letter but to go to Mary and explain the matter face to face. Lincoln accepted this advice and called upon Mary and presumably this call took place on that fatal first of January.

One can imagine that scene in the Edwards parlor: the tall young man with pained face and halting speech beginning to tell the pretty, happy-faced girl that their romance and dreams were at an end, explaining to her why it was best for the engagement to be broken. Possibly he reproached her for her light behavior in flirting with another man — that may have been the fuse which set off his vast accumulation of misgivings. One can picture the dawning incredulity in her blue eyes, the commencing quiver of her lips. According to Joshua's account, she sprang from her chair, burst into tears, and cried out brokenly: ". . . the deceiver shall be deceived wo is me." Her words seem to indicate that something she had done in the flirting line was on her conscience.

What does any man do when he sees the woman he loves in tears and anguish of spirit? With his own eyes wet, Mr. Lincoln took Mary into his arms and drew her upon his lap to kiss away those tears. His dark shaggy head bent contritely above the bright chestnut hair, his weathered cheek was close to hers, soft and tear-stained. It is a rare and intimate picture of the lovers at that dramatic moment when their new-found and tender love was crossed by fate.

The response of passionate arms and lips does not go well with a man's using cold logic to explain to the girl sitting on his lap the reasons why they should not get married. Lincoln comforted his little Molly as best he could and then abruptly took his departure, leaving the situation between them up in the air. It is possible they were interrupted. For all that is known, sister Elizabeth may have heard Mary's startled outcry and walked in. At all events, Mrs. Edwards soon knew what had happened and seized her opportunity and used her older-sister influence to make sure that the estrangement was complete and permanent.

It was said that she insisted that Mary write Mr. Lincoln a letter releasing him from the engagement. The girl could hardly do otherwise, but she put one thing in that letter which one may be sure was not authorized by sister Elizabeth: she wrote Mr. Lincoln that her feeling for him remained unchanged and she stood ready to renew the engagement. It was a remarkable admission for a proud young woman of the Victorian era. That she could do so shows that Mr. Lincoln's reasons for asking to be released did not offend her. If he had told her he did not love her or that he loved another, she would have cut off her hand before she would have written this. But if he told her that he was poor and could not take care of her as she was used to being taken care of and that the Edwardses (including Ninian, who considered that he had certain rights because she was his ward) were against the marriage, her love and pride would not have been offended. If he mentioned her flirting, she doubtless realized she had been wrong in deceiving him about her true feelings. Mary could be counted on in the end to acknowledge her own faults.

As to his love for her, that quick embrace and his kisses, his tenderness at her tears told her more eloquently than words all she needed to know about that. She had too often seen that light in his eyes when he looked at her. Any girl knows by a dozen unspoken evidences whether she has a man's heart when she has been engaged to him. It is possible Mary had even more positive assurance. One garbled account of the incident does say that Dr. Henry, devoted friend of both the lovers who was tending Mr. Lincoln in his agonized state, went to Mary and explained the condition Lincoln was in, and that it was then that the girl wrote him the letter telling him she still loved him.

Lincoln's feelings were tearing him to pieces. He was caught in a cruel dilemma from which he saw no honorable way out. He had won Mary's love and entered into an agreement to marry her. His lawyer's training as well as his scrupulous conscience made him respect a contract and yet he had asked that it be broken. On the other hand, fathers and guardians had their recognized rights. How could he marry the girl when her family thought he would make her unhappy? He had so few things upon which to pride himself, but among these things was his integrity. Yet no course of action was open to a man with his torturing conscience that left that integrity unviolated.

There was another factor. It is recalled that hypochondria involves the idea of exaggerated anxiety over one's health. Joshua Speed wrote later that Lincoln was so worried over his physical condition at this time that he wrote an eminent physician in another state describing his ailment and asking advice. The physician refused to prescribe without a personal examination. A conscientious man filled with dark doubts about his health does not feel it would be fair to a girl to marry her until he knows what is the matter and can be assured of getting over it.

So much for reason and conscience, but the emotional agony was even worse. No one questions what it means to a man to find the woman he loves and wishes to marry: life takes on a joyous new focus and vitality. This was especially true of Mr. Lincoln, whose early meager existence had contained little demonstration of affection. When this chosen woman, young, pretty, desirable, gives him ardent love in return and promises to marry him, he walks in a golden haze. Suddenly this sweet, newly discovered world was shattered. Mr. Lincoln had barely tasted the joy of having someone of his very own to love when that joy was taken from him, leaving him in a gray and flavorless world.

The gossiping tongues were right insofar as they said Mr. Lincoln was lovesick. It is a malady akin to but even more devastating than homesickness. He was missing Mary terribly. Through all their married life ran evidences that he wanted her with him. Again Mr. Conkling gives a close-up view, a new bit of evidence. The April after the Lincoln marriage when the lawyers went on their semiannual pilgrimage of the judicial circuit Mr. Conkling journeyed to Bloomington. From there he wrote Mercy: "Found Lincoln desperately homesick and turning his face frequently toward the south." South to Springfield, where his bride was then living in one room at the Globe Tavern and looking forward to the birth of their first baby.

He was homesick now for Molly, Molly who was interested in all the little things that happened to him, who met his self-doubting with buoyant confidence, who had made him the center of her world. She had furnished the color and "variety" of life without which it had suddenly become "exceedingly tasteless" to him.

There was no thought to which the tormented man could turn for comfort. Mary had given him her love and he had made her unhappy. As he was to write shortly, that thought killed his very soul. He could not even wish to be cheerful when she was unhappy. In such mental perturbation thoughts go in circles; how could he, poor and in debt, make her happy if he married her? All the reasons he had given Miss Owens as to why she should not marry him applied doubly to Mary, who loved the trimmings of life. And he could remember Miss Owens had told him bluntly that he would not make a kind and considerate husband. That lady had contributed to his self-doubting. All the old humiliation of that fiasco of a wooing would naturally come back to lacerate his sensitized feelings.

So one may interpret the thoughts of "the most miserable man living." Mrs. Edwards, even if she did not understand Mr. Lincoln, seems to have understood the situation very well. "Mr Lincoln loved Mary," were her words, "he went crazy in my own opinion — not because he loved Miss Edwards as said, but because he wanted to marry and doubted his ability & capacity to please and support a wife."

A person who feels he has enough mental misery to distribute to the whole human race is not in a healthy mood to see matters straight. Lincoln began to question the institution of marriage itself, as to whether it was the Elysium pictured by the sentimentalists of the day. He questioned his own love for Mary; was it great enough to surmount all the problems, the delicate adjustments, and basic changes in living that marriage would bring? Traces of the marriage shyness he had shown in regard to Miss Owens came back to him.

On January 19, the crisis of his illness over, Mr. Lincoln, pale, weak, and emaciated, appeared in the legislature and from then on attended faithfully, taking an active part in its work. On February 5 he tried to give a boost to his rival, Mr. Webb, by writing a letter suggesting him for District Attorney. One wonders whether he was nobly trying to do his rival a good turn in case this suitor of Molly's were able to console her and thus wipe out her unhappiness.

On March 5 Mary's cousin and Lincoln's law partner, Mr. Stuart, recommended that he be appointed Chargé d'Affaires at Bogotá. Again questions arise: was Mr. Stuart trying to get his unhappy partner a change of scene or was he trying to get the man whom the family considered undesirable for Mary away from Springfield? He could have had both motives. Certainly the fact that the moody Mr. Lincoln could get into a state of such utter misery that he was "unable to attend to any bussiness" was not calculated to increase in Mr. Stuart's mind his desirability either as a law partner or as a prospective husband. Somehow one is not too surprised to find that in the spring of '41 the Stuart & Lincoln partnership was dissolved and Mr. Lincoln moved what legal equipment he had over to the office of Stephen T. Logan. Again he was the junior partner. Mr. Stuart consolidated the family forces by taking Ninian's brother Benjamin S. Edwards in with him.

April as usual brought the spring round of the Illinois

towns on the judicial circuit. Probably never before or afterward was Mr. Lincoln so glad to leave Springfield and start out. It was a way of life he loved: crossing the prairie by horseback or homemade vehicle, putting up at lonely farmhouses or village inns where the lawyers slept two in a bed and perhaps eight in a room, holding court in the little towns to match wits over small legal and human problems, exchanging news and funny stories in man's talk on sidewalk or in tavern. The little villages, isolated because of the lack of railroads and other means of communication, welcomed the travelers with open arms and held carnival for a day or two, giving parties and entertainments for the visitors.

It is difficult today to picture what was involved in those lonely journeyings across the wild land between towns. As a fellow lawyer and friend of Mr. Lincoln said, the prairies, later under cultivation and teeming with a busy life, were "then quite as desolate and almost as solitary as at Creation's dawn." Mr. Conkling also traveled the circuit and he wrote to his beloved Mercy a fascinating description of such a journey. To meet another traveler was such a rare event that the stranger, in the emotional release of hearing a human voice again, was apt to feel an undue sense of intimacy and ask questions about one's income, occupation, residence, present business and future prospects. If you did not answer, continued Mr. Conkling, you might be suspected as a horse thief.

Losing one's way was a common experience and night sometimes overtook one far from human habitation. James told Mercy of a "provoking situation" in which he once found himself: "in a small house on the edge of a . . . prairie — with a plenty of cold, without fire, tea without cream and bread without butter [perhaps it was corn dodger], with some two or three crying noisy children about you and by no means a prepossessing landlady." When he looked out, all he saw was the road stretching before him as far as eye could reach "and a dark heavy cloud extending directly over it and pouring down the rain for hours upon it."

At another stop he was treated more hospitably; a fire was made up "in the parlor, decorated with festoons of yarn and arranged in the most approved sucker style with its creaking bedsteads, broken chairs and cracked tables." Here the food was good and James, with his "chin just at edge of the table," had no difficulty scraping it directly into his mouth "with the blade of a broken knife." He slept in the loft that night, though just why he did not rate one of those creaking bedsteads in the parlor one does not know. Doubtless in either place he would have had plenty of sleeping company.

Conditions like these, along with miserable roads, deep sloughs in which a buggy mired down, broken shafts and lost linchpins, spring floods, swollen streams, drenching rains (perhaps at times an unseasonable blizzard), and high winds, were what Lincoln encountered when he went traveling on the circuit. One hopes he had the company of fellow lawyers as he rode across the prairies in the spring of 1841; their loneliness and dreariness were too much in harmony with his own melancholy thoughts.

CHAPTER 11

Mr. Lincoln Writes a Murder Mystery

SPRINGFIELD was full of faithful correspondents who kept absent friends informed of the news. By May Mrs. William Butler, who took a kind and affectionate interest in Mr. Lincoln — as a motherly woman would with a lovable young man who ate his meals daily at her table — had written to Joshua Speed that her boarder was "on the mend." He was also her lodger now, as he had moved over to the Butler home after Joshua left town. Joshua wrote back to her husband how glad he was that Lincoln was getting over his melancholia and then it is revealed that he, Joshua, was also subject to hypochondria: "Say to her [Mrs. Butler] that I have had one attack since I left Springfield. . . . I am not as happy as I could be and yet so much happier than I deserve to be that I think I ought to be satisfied." Joshua was soon to rival Lincoln as the most miserable man living; his introspection was destined to give him a terrible time with himself. But this letter shows that Lincoln was coming out of his "blues."

Providentially for the enjoyment and stimulation of Springfield, as the talk about the broken engagement and Mr. Lincoln's acting "crazy" died down, a new and thrilling topic arose. Early in June the town was electrified by a

murder mystery. One can picture little groups of men talking excitedly on the four streets that bounded the square
and housewives equally wrought up speculating about it
over the back fence.

Mr. Lincoln, with no sign of mental depression but with
humor and consummate storytelling skill, wrote on June 19
a full account of it to Joshua. He was in a position to know
what he was talking about, as he was one of the lawyers
who defended the accused.

"We have had the highest state of excitement here for a
week past that our community has ever witnessed . . ."
began his letter to "Dear Speed." "The chief personages in
the drama, are Archibald Fisher, supposed to be murdered;
and Archibald Trailor, Henry Trailor, and William
Trailor, supposed to have murdered him." The three Trailors were brothers living at some distance from each other,
Archibald at Springfield, Henry at Clary's Grove, about
twenty miles northwest, and William in Warren County,
more than a hundred miles distant in the same direction.
Fisher, a carpenter and odd-job man without a family, had
been living at William Trailor's home.

The four men came to Springfield one Monday to stay
overnight. When the brothers assembled for supper that
evening after touring the metropolis, Fisher was unaccount-
ably missing. Search was made for him without success and
on Tuesday Henry and William Trailor had to start back to
their homes without him. Henry and his neighbors, however, were worried and came back to Springfield to search
again and finally advertised his disappearance in the paper.

The town became aware of the case of the missing carpenter.

Some days went by and then the postmaster at Springfield received a startling letter from the postmaster in Warren County stating that William had arrived home "and was telling a verry mysterious and improbable story about the disappearance of Fisher, which induced the community there to suppose that he had been disposed of unfairly." William was boasting that Fisher was dead and had willed him his money.

When this letter was made public, as Lincoln wrote, it "immediately set the whole town and adjoining country agog. . . ." Everybody began to search for the body with great thoroughness, cellars and wells were examined, dead dogs and horses were dug up, fresh human graves were pried into. A deputy sheriff was dispatched to Warren County to arrest William.

At this point the plot thickened. Henry was fetched from Clary's Grove by a deputy sheriff "and showed an evident inclination to insinuate that he knew Fisher to be dead, and that Arch: & Wm. had killed him." Henry "guessed" the body could be found in Spring Creek not far from "Hickoxes mill." "Away the People swept like a herd of buffaloes," continued Mr. Lincoln, "and cut down Hickoxes mill dam *nolens volens,* to draw the water out of the pond; and then went up and down, and down and up the creek, fishing and raking, and ducking and diving for two days. . . ." Everyone except Mr. Hickox had a wonderful time, but no dead body was found.

In the meantime a place in the brush had been found where there were signs of a struggle. "From this scuffle ground, was the sign of something about the size of a man having been dragged to the edge of the thicket, where it joined the track of some small wheeled carriage which was drawn by one horse, as shown by the horse tracks." One can imagine the excitement when it was discovered that the carriage tracks led off toward Spring Creek.

Near this "drag trail" Dr. Merryman, in true Sherlock Holmes fashion, "found *two hairs*, which after a long scientific examination, he pronounced to be triangular human hairs. . . ." Like a true scientist he went thoroughly into the subject of how many kinds of human hair there were and came up with the judgment "that these two were of the whiskers, because the ends were cut, showing they had flourished in the neighborhood of the razor's opperations."

Matters progressed to the point where all three of the Trailor brothers had been arrested and put in jail. On Friday, June 18, a legal examination was held before two justices at which Mr. Lincoln with his new senior law partner Mr. Logan and another lawyer friend defended the accused.

Much evidence was listened to which pointed more and more to a dark crime. Henry Trailor was introduced by the prosecution and gave a most circumstantial account of what had happened when he and his brothers left Springfield. When they got out of town, he, Henry, was placed as sentinel to watch that no one approached while William and Archibald "took the dearborn out of the road a small distance to the edge of the thicket, where they stopped, and he saw them lift the body of a man into it; that they then moved off with the carriage in the direction of Hickoxes mill, and he loitered about for something like an hour when William returned with the carriage, but without Arch: and said that they had put *him* in a safe place. . . ." One can imagine the excitement of the listeners and their glances at Mr. Lincoln and others of the defense at this damaging evidence. Henry proved more and more satisfactory to the prosecution as he continued: "William told him, that he and Arch: had killed Fisher the evening before; that the way they did it was by him (William) knocking him down with a club, and Arch: then choking him to death."

That seemed to settle it and doubtless thoughts of mob violence were seething in the minds of some of the listeners. Then the defense produced an unexpected witness and a great deflation followed. This star witness was a physician from Warren County, a Dr. Gilmore, and his evidence proved the "*murderee*" was not dead! Dr. Gilmore informed the court that on the very day on which William Trailor was arrested, Fisher had appeared at his house, apparently very unwell and unable to account for his movements. The physician explained that Fisher had once received a head injury which made him subject to occasional temporary derangements. The man was still so sick that Dr. Gilmore had not dared bring him along to Springfield. The witness had made a hurried and strenuous journey, "riding all evening and all night," in order to get to the trial in time; his patient could not have stood the rigors of such traveling.

The prosecution, of course, did not take this demolishing

of their case lying down; they raised questions whether the doctor's story was not a fabrication. Unimpeachable witnesses, however, swore to the physician's "good character for truth and veracity." The defense won and the Trailors were discharged. There had been no murder. On the following Monday, Fisher, as Lincoln wrote elsewhere, appeared in Springfield "in full life and proper person."

So what happened remains a mystery and one is left free to speculate. Did a talent for tall tales and vivid imagination run in the Trailor family? Did Archibald and William go through the pantomime of hiding a body with a dummy as a sort of rough joke to fool their brother Henry? He was "about forty yards distant" from them. At all events, right after the trial "Henry still protested that no power on earth could ever show Fisher alive," while the other two brothers were sure he would be found living, as testified, at the doctor's. Archibald and William never offered an explanation and Henry later would not speak of the subject.

An elaborate theory as to what happened has been suggested: Fisher, owing to his head injury, might have had a seizure or fit which left him in an unconscious state resembling death. Archibald and William, either being with him or finding him, might have been fearful that they would be accused of murder and therefore tried to conceal the body. It is even suggested that they took him in their carriage to the millpond and dumped him in, where the cold water revived him and he climbed out. But if this theory is correct, why did the two brothers tell Henry they had killed Fisher, going into circumstantial details? Would they not instead have told him of their fear of being accused of murder, so as to put him on his guard in what he said? So much for speculation.

Mr. Lincoln in his letter to Joshua did full justice to the comical effect when the idea of a murder was exploded. "When the doctor's story was first made public," he wrote, "it was amusing to scan and contemplate the countenances, and hear the remarks of those who had been actively engaged in the search for the dead body. Some looked quizical, some melancholly, and some furiously angry." One man who had been very active swore that he knew all along that Fisher was not dead "and that *he* had not stirred an inch to hunt for him;" another "who had taken the lead in cuting down Hickoxes mill dam, and wanted to hang Hickox for objecting, looked most awfully wo-begone; he seemed the '*wictim of hunrequited haffection*' as represented in the comic almanic we used to laugh over; and Hart, the little drayman that hauled Molly home once, said it was too *damned* bad, to have so much trouble and no hanging after all."

This letter shows not only that Mr. Lincoln was able to attend to business (and storytelling) in a most competent manner, but also that he had come out of his melancholia and recovered his sense of humor. Underneath, however, he continued to be in a distressed and worried state of mind.

Perhaps it should be added that for all its excitability Springfield's heart was in the right place. Shortly after Lincoln's letter was written the citizens held a meeting to express to their fellow townsman, Archibald Trailor, their apologies and regrets that they had believed him involved in a murder. Yet, as Lincoln himself pointed out, if Fisher had not been found alive, "it is difficult to conceive what could have saved the Trailors from the consequence of having murdered him."

Once again the story arrives at a rich oasis of evidence in a letter written by Mary herself which was mailed to Mercy Levering the day before Lincoln composed his story of the murder mystery. One can go into the Edwards home on the hill and find out how Miss Todd was holding up in this estrangement from her lover and what thoughts were occupying her mind.

She shows much more restraint in expressing her mood than Mr. Lincoln did, but the letter opens in a minor key and she admits that she has a "sad spirit." She apologizes for not writing her "own dear Merce" sooner, but she feared she would inflict a letter that was "flat, stale & unprofitable." She almost indulges in the prevalent soul searching when she says: "Why I have not written oftener appears strange even to *me*, who should best know *myself*, that most difficult of all problems to solve."

If Mr. Lincoln missed Mary and was homesick for her, was she likewise homesick to see him? "The last two or three months have been of *interminable* length," she wrote. "After my gay companions of last winter departed, I was left much to the solitude of my own thoughts, and some *lingering regrets* over the past, which time can alone overshadow with its healing balm." That time's balm had not accomplished much yet is suggested by several disclosures in the letter. She continues: "Summer in all its beauty has again come, the prairie land looks as beautiful as it did in the olden time, when we strolled together & derived so much of happiness from each other's society — this is past & more than this."

If one has been wondering what were Mr. Webb's chances of getting Molly on the rebound, here is the answer: "The *winning widower*," she says, is not seen around anymore. Nor was he "winning" as far as she was concerned. Merce had been under the wrong impression: "In your last, you appeared impressed with the prevalent idea that we were *dearer* to each other than friends. The idea was neither new nor strange, dear Merce, the knowing world, have coupled our names together for months past, merely through the folly & belief of another, who strangely imagined we were attached to each other."

That last sentence gives one pause. Could "another" refer to Mr. Lincoln? Could he have resented Mr. Webb's attentions to Mary and misinterpreted the situation between them? There was evidently a case of flirting on Mary's conscience. Was the torture of jealousy added to the other factors contributing to Mr. Lincoln's great distress of mind? Was there hidden meaning in what his wife was to write him before the decade of the forties was over: a teasing threat to "carry on quite a flirtation" with Mr. Webb? She added that he (Mr. Lincoln) knew "*we*, always had a *penchant* that way." It is an interesting speculation.

One knows conclusively from what follows in Mary's letter to Merce that Mr. Webb earnestly wooed Mary and what her answer was: "In your friendly & confiding ear allow me to whisper that my *heart can never be his.* I have deeply regretted that his constant visits, attentions &c

should have given room for remarks, which were to me unpleasant." There was a "difference of some eighteen or
twenty summers" in their ages and Mary had learned what
the companionship of a congenial man could mean to her;
with Mr. Webb she did not have that "congeneality of
feeling, without which I should never feel justifiable in re-
signing my happiness into the safe keeping of another, even
should that other be, far too worthy for me, with his two
sweet little objections." Mary loved children, but it was not
her plan to be a stepmother.

Of course she reported to Merce on "*Jacob Faithful.*"
She had seen him at a neighbor's one evening recently "and
in one quiet sequestered nook in the room he was seated,
sad & lonely. No doubt his thoughts were busy with you &
the past."

It appears that the lovely Matilda Edwards who had arrived at the Edwards home for a "visit" the November before was still there in the middle of June. With such warm
mutual affection between them, one wonders whether
Mary was as confidential with Matilda as she was with
Mercy. Mary needed a confidante to talk to during these
lonely months of separation from the man she loved and it
emphatically could not be her sister Elizabeth.

Another bit of news was that Mr. Speed was still in Kentucky and occasionally he wrote to her. With the mention
of Joshua the girl reached the subject which was nearest her
heart. It was so sensitive a topic she could not bring herself
to write Mr. Lincoln's name; he is brought into the letter
by way of Mr. Speed: "*His* worthy friend, deems me un-
worthy of notice, as I have not met *him* in the gay world

for months. With the usual comfort of misery, [I] imagine that others were as seldom gladdened by his presence as my humble self, yet I would that the case were different, that he would once more resume his station in Society, that 'Richard should be himself again,' much, much happiness would it afford me." Shyly and delicately she has revealed her own heart, its "misery" and longing for her lover, her yearning that he could be his old self again, that things could be restored to the time when they two had walked together in the sweetness and glory of their first betrothal.

CHAPTER 12

Tangled Emotions of Two Gentlemen

MR. Lincoln had concluded his murder-mystery letter to Joshua with the statement: "I stick to my promise to come to Louisville." After four years of affectionate companionship, separation was hard on these two friends and a plan for Lincoln to visit Speed in Kentucky and for Joshua to return to Springfield with him had been afoot for some time.

But the lawyer had his living to make and it was difficult for him to take time off for mere visiting. Legal business kept him busy until he left for the South the second week in August. The slow-motion journey by horse and steamboat took approximately a week.

At the end of that journey was a way of living new to the man who had grown up in a log cabin. The fact that the plantation of the Speed family, situated a few miles out of Louisville, had its own name, Farmington, gives some indication of its character. The dignified red brick house with beautiful portico and doorway stood on a slight rise of ground. From the rear veranda, where perhaps the two friends were to sit together in the summer evenings, one could view a long peaceful sweep of Kentucky acres. For the first time in his life Lincoln became acquainted with luxurious leisure and with what must have been equally impressive to him, the Southerner's aptitude for enjoying leisure. The slave quarters, set far back in the rear, furnished servants for every household task, including bringing coffee to a visiting gentleman's bedroom in the mornings. To this particular visitor that must have seemed a strange height of luxury. Perhaps some things in this visit were to make him understand better Molly's background and pleasure-loving temperament.

Joshua undoubtedly met Lincoln when his boat docked at Louisville. One likes to imagine the reunion between these two, their fervent handclasps and glowing faces (with more said by the young men's eyes than their lips), and the arrival at the plantation, where Joshua introduced his guest to his mother, his sister Mary, and others of the family. They were wholesome and delightful people and soon grew fond of the appealing young lawyer from Illinois.

He is shortly found doing very well for a gentleman who had felt repressed and ill at ease with some of Springfield's fine ladies, like Mrs. Edwards. He and Mary Speed soon became, to use his own words, "something of cronies" and once there was a bit of romping and teasing between them that went to the point where, as he wrote her afterwards, "I . . . was under the necessity of shutting you up in a room to prevent your committing an assault and battery upon me. . . ."

At Joshua's Old Kentucky Home Lincoln found all the desirable features mentioned in the wistful lines of the song: 'Twas summer, the darkies were gay, the corn-tops were ripe and the meadows were in bloom. The days unfolded pleasantly for the visitor. He rode to town in the Speed carriage, he visited the law office of Joshua's brother James (whom he one day as President would appoint Attorney General of the United States), he played with Eliza Davis, a little girl of the family who was visiting at Farmington. Best of all he could resume with Joshua those intimate, confidential discussions about people, religion, marriage, and things in general.

Joshua, one is not surprised to learn, had fallen in love again, this time with a beautiful dark-eyed girl named Fanny Henning. She lived with her uncle, a gentleman who took his politics seriously, not to say violently. The result was that when Joshua called for the purpose of wooing the niece, he found himself instead forced to talk politics with Uncle. Lincoln, learning the situation, undertook an assignment after his own heart. He went with his friend to see Fanny and one can imagine the grave face and huge enjoyment with which he took issue with Uncle on certain touchy matters of politics. In the ensuing prolonged and heated argument Joshua had ample opportunity to devote himself to the girl.

Lincoln was pleased with Fanny; he thought she was "one of the sweetest girls in the world." There was only one thing he could wish otherwise about her; he thought she had "something of a tendency to melancholly." One can understand why he who suffered so much from "the blues" would not enjoy a similar indulgence in anyone else. It was certainly to be said in Molly's favor that she was by nature cheerful, inclined to look on the bright side of things, and knew how to enjoy herself.

Though he had himself well in hand, he still suffered at times from extreme depression. It did not help matters that he developed a terrific toothache and had to go to the city to have the offender removed. The crude dentistry of the time failed to get the tooth out after efforts which must have been excruciating. Pain had largely to be taken raw in that rugged age. (After he returned to Illinois a more strong-armed operator tore out the tooth, "bringing with it a bit of the jawbone," as he wrote Mary Speed later, "the consequence of which is that my mouth is now so sore that I can neither talk, nor eat. I am litterally 'subsisting on savoury remembrances' — that is, being unable to eat, I am living upon the remembrance of the delicious dishes of peaches and cream we used to have at your house.")

Lincoln was never to know peace of mind during the estrangement from Mary. Joshua's mother gave him a Bible, saying it was "the best cure for the 'Blues' . . ." and he intended "to read it regularly," he wrote later. He carried out that intention the rest of his life. In the White House during the Civil War at a moment when the military outlook for the Union seemed unutterably dark, he reached for the Bible and read in the Book of Job to recover his poise and courage to go on.

He appreciated Mrs. Speed's present. Twenty years later when he was President he sent her his picture with an inscription over his signature reminding her of this gift she had given him so long before, a thoughtful act in an overworked man and one that does not jibe very well with Mrs. Edwards's description of him as one who "was a little ungrateful . . . for the want of recollection."

Leaving the Speed family was hard. Lincoln, whom Mrs. Edwards thought so cold he could love nothing, gave all the household at Farmington his warm affection. In his letter to Mary Speed he mentioned each one: "Is little Siss Eliza Davis at your house yet? If she is kiss her 'o'er and o'er again' for me." He remembered the "happy face" of one of the sisters, he put in a message for Joshua's mother, he sent his "verry highest regard" to Fanny Henning.

Joshua kept his promise to return to Springfield with his friend. "We got on board the Steam Boat Lebanon, in the locks of the Canal about 12. o'clock. M. of the day we left," Lincoln wrote back to Joshua's sister. That was at Louisville on Tuesday, September 7, and it was evening the following Monday when they reached St. Louis. The *Lebanon* was a comparatively small boat and Lincoln was vexed at the delays caused by getting stuck on sand bars.

But one scene on board was etched on his mind. He watched with deep thought and compassion a group of twelve Negro slaves who were being taken to work in the fields of the deep South. They were chained together "precisely like so many fish upon a trot-line," he wrote, and "were being separated forever from the scenes of their childhood, their friends, their fathers and mothers . . . and going into perpetual slavery where the lash of the master is proverbially more ruthless and unrelenting than any other. . . ." And yet he observed: "They were the most cheerful and apparantly happy creatures on board." One "played the fiddle almost continually, and the others danced, sung, cracked jokes. . . ."

The sight of these victims of slavery was a "continual

torment" both to his moral sense and his tender pity. It made him miserable. He tried to console himself with the reflection that " 'God tempers the wind to the shorn lamb,' or in other words, that He renders the worst of human conditions tolerable, while He permits the best, to be nothing better than tolerable." There is a bit of growing-up here. Human happiness is never a perfect thing; one must give up the thought of achieving the ideal by a forced compromise with things as they are. This is a discovery it is always hard for young idealism to take.

Lincoln and Joshua were both having great difficulty adjusting themselves to the *status quo* in religion and marriage. Joshua, who remained in Springfield until the beginning of the following year, 1842, was in a dither over his love affair. He poured out all his fears, his melancholia, and nervous sensations to his friend. Lincoln, who had passed through just such a period of mental misery a few months before and had at least got hold of himself, though he had not solved his own problem, was making a passionate effort to bolster up Joshua through his mental funk. In effect he was turning himself into a psychiatrist in order to help his friend.

There had evidently been much discussion between these two self-analytical young men when Joshua, his visit to Springfield over, departed for Kentucky to continue his courtship and winning of Fanny Henning. Lincoln wrote a letter for him to take along with him as a sort of treatment when he got into the depths of depression.

Now comes that remarkable group of letters, those in which Abraham Lincoln in his young manhood laid bare his inmost feelings and those of Joshua Speed. One can go into the troubled minds of these two at the high peak of emotional life when both had fallen in love and with the aid of considerable introspection and ratiocination had succeeded in tying themselves up into psychological knots.

The letter Lincoln handed Joshua as the latter left for Kentucky began: "Feeling, as you know I do, the deepest solicitude for the success of the enterprize you are engaged in, I adopt this as the last method I can invent to aid you, in case (which God forbid) you shall need any aid." He explained that if he had merely said these things orally, he was afraid Joshua would forget them at the very time he needed them most. "As I think it reasonable that you will feel verry badly some time between this and the final consummation of your purpose, it is intended that you shall read this just at such a time."

Joshua's low state of mind is indicated in Lincoln's expressions describing it: "present affliction," "melancholly bodings," "agony of despondency." Something "indescribably horrible and alarming" haunted Joshua and Lincoln feared his friend would die if he did not get some relief from this "immense suffering." These expressions might have been used for Abraham exactly one year before. As he advises his friend and analyzes his condition, one gets Lincoln's description in retrospect of his own thoughts and reasoning when he had been "the most miserable man living." There is also a suggestion of the methods by which he worked himself out of his depression to the point of resuming a normal life.

As was characteristic of him in approaching a problem, he went into it thoroughly and logically. Joshua felt so "verry badly . . . because of *three special causes*, added to the *general one*," which was that he was "*naturally of a nervous temperament. . . .*" He was so sensitive that things affected him with far more than average force. "It is out of this, that the painful difference between you and the mass of the world springs."

Lincoln's letter continued: "The first special cause is, *your exposure to bad weather* on your journey, which my experience clearly proves to be verry severe on defective nerves." There is a significant admission in the last two words. Lincoln considered that he also was one of those nervous or sensitive ones to whom the pressures of living are at times unbearable. There is also a hint of the fatigue and frazzling which he had often experienced from the roughness and exposure, the long-drawn-out hardship of the traveling he was forced to do.

The second special cause of Joshua's trouble was "*the absence of all business and conversation of friends*" which might divert his mind. Lincoln knew what he was talking about; in the melancholia which followed his broken engagement he had found it hard to attend to business and had avoided social assemblies.

The third special cause was "*the rapid and near approach of that crisis on which all your thoughts and feelings concentrate.*" Joshua was heading toward marriage and was beset with doubts and fears about love and the state of matrimony. Lincoln was just the man to deal with that subject: "I know what the painful point with you is, at all times when you are unhappy. It is an apprehension that you do not love her as you should."

Lincoln had suffered from that same apprehension. It had been one of those painful doubts which had beaten a track round and round in his sore and tortured mind. Perhaps it was this he meant when in this same letter he spoke of "that *intensity* of thought, which will some times wear the sweetest idea thread-bare and turn it to the bitterness of death." It is a sentence which shows that the prairie lawyer was becoming a literary artist.

He had learned how to answer Joshua's apprehension that he did not sufficiently love Fanny. "What nonsense!" he exclaimed. "How came you to court her? Was it because you thought she desired it; and that you had given her reason to expect it?" That reason would apply to "at least twenty others of whom you can think. . . ." Had Joshua courted her for her wealth? "Why, you knew she had none. But you say you *reasoned* yourself *into* it. What do you mean by that? Was it not, that you found yourself unable to *reason* yourself *out* of it? Did you not think, and partly form the purpose, of courting her the first time you ever saw or heard of her?" What had reason to do with it at that early stage? Joshua knew very little about her then except "her *personal appearance and deportment*; and these, if they impress at all, impress the *heart* and not the head."

Had not Abraham's eyes followed the pretty figure of Molly when first he met her, had he not gazed as if fascinated on her sparkling face? He had not been reasoning at those moments that a girl with her background was hardly a suitable match for a poor man like himself.

"Say candidly," continued this man of experience to Fanny's suitor, "were not those heavenly *black eyes*, the whole basis of all your early *reasoning* on the subject?"

Lawyerlike he piled up his arguments to prove Joshua's love for Fanny. "What earthly consideration would you take to find her scouting and despising you, and giving herself up to another?" Again one wonders if Mr. Lincoln had not suffered the pangs of jealousy of Mr. Douglas or Mr. Webb as he added: "But of this you have no apprehension; and therefore you can not bring it home to your feelings."

Such was the letter of psychiatric advice which Lincoln handed Joshua when he left Springfield at the beginning of 1842, a year which was to be a momentous one. The lawyer concluded with intense concern and affection: "I shall be so anxious about you, that I want you to write me every mail."

CHAPTER **13**

"That Still Kills My Soul"

THIS is the love story of Mary and Abraham. But the searchlight turned on them has caught in the outer circle of illumination some other lovers of most endearing qualities. Considering how helpful they have been, it is the least one can do to inquire whether "Jacob Faithful" and his "Dear Mercy" were finally married to live happily ever after.

Miss Levering became the bride of Mr. Conkling in September 1841. Mary probably had mingled feelings about the event, affectionate joy and interest in their happiness and secret pain at the contrast in fortune between herself and her friend. Mercy was being united to the man she loved while she, Mary, was not even seeing the one to whom she had given her heart.

If friends at the wedding festivities repeated the wish which Mr. Conkling himself had expressed at the Abell wedding, "Peace and Happiness be with them," a letter written jointly by the Conklings, apparently about a year and a half after their marriage, answers the question as to whether that wish came true. The picture this letter presents takes one into Springfield on a winter night "as dark as a cloudy sky and black soil can make it." Mr. and Mrs.

James Conkling were cozily at home, where Mercy was writing a letter to her mother. The hour arriving when she had planned to go to a sewing society, she asked her husband to finish the letter for her. He dutifully took up the pen and wrote: "I have just deposited Merse in the bottom of a large farm waggon and seated her as comfortably as circumstances would permit in a bundle of hay where several of the members were already partly hid." As he continued, it is seen how youth and gaiety made a frolic of primitive conditions, mud, and cold. "They drive on to the next house, where they pick up a few more passengers and so on in succession, till they cluster together as thick as bees in a hive." The young husband continued delightfully: "I fancy now I can see them piled across each other and stowed as close as crockery ware, while with their merry peals of laughter and merriment they are carried on to the '*Society*' Here if not *dumped* miscellaneously in the mud yet, in the scramble & effort to disentangle themselves and appropriate to their own use the members that properly belong to each, they come as near to it as comfort and convenience will permit."

James confesses that this is the first time Mercy has ever deliberately left him to spend an evening alone. Heroically he says he does not mind this too much once in eighteen months, but adds the hope that she will come home early. He proves himself a tactful son-in-law; he tells Mercy's mother how faithfully the girl "carries into practice the wise old maxims" she has been taught at home. "That '*Ma does so and so*' is indisputable authority and what '*Pa used to tell us gals*' is at once adopted as a rule."

James gives an appealing description of his young wife. According to his gaily boasting account, she can do everything much better than anyone else; no one can design a costume, fit a bonnet, arrange a supper table, "fit a stock so neatly and rig it up with a little bow," or cook as expertly as she can. "The lover of chicken salad knows not when to stop his attention to her dishes and an epicure would surfeit himself over her delicious preserves."

One begins to suspect he is writing more for Mercy's perusal than for her mother's. The suspicion grows as he continues: "Withal she is blessed with a considerable share of that characteristic and commendable modesty which always accompanies true merit, genius and talent and I have no doubt in the world that when she returns and reads this panegyric upon her virtues, she will attempt to blush most deeply, and declare that I have spoiled her letter." He added with a twinkle: "We shall see — " At this point Mercy returned, blushed pinkly on reading what he had written, and declared it was all "a downright story."

Lincoln's next letter to Joshua was written early in February 1842. In the meantime Fanny had become ill and Joshua, in terrible anxiety, had written his adviser Lincoln a frantic letter of "melancholly bodings as to her early death." Lincoln answered it on the very day it came: "You well know that I do not feel my own sorrows much more keenly than I do yours . . . and yet I assure you I was not much hurt by what you wrote me of your excessively bad feeling at the time you wrote. . . . because I hope and believe, that your present anxiety and distress about *her* health and *her* life, must and will forever banish those horid doubts, which I know you sometimes felt, as to the truth of your affection for her."

Lincoln almost considered, he said, that the Almighty had sent this present affliction to Joshua for the express purpose of removing those doubts. He hoped that Fanny, by the time his letter arrived, would be much improved. "It really appears to me that you yourself ought to rejoice, and not sorrow, at this indubitable evidence of your undying affection for her. Why Speed, if you did not love her, although you might not wish her death, you would most calmly be resigned to it." He added with that great sensitivity of his: "Perhaps this point is no longer a question with you, and my pertenacious dwelling upon it, is a rude intrusion upon your feelings. If so, you must pardon me. You know the Hell I have suffered on that point, and how tender I am upon it. You know I do not mean wrong."

Lincoln reported cheerfully on his own condition: "I have been quite clear of hypo since you left, — even better than I was along in the fall." He wanted an immediate answer to this letter.

He got it and it contained good news. Joshua and Fanny were to be married February 15. Since letters, like travelers, moved very slowly, by the time Lincoln could get an answer back to Kentucky, the wedding would have taken place. It gave him a queer pang that the relation between Joshua and himself would be changed now; there would never again be the cherished companionship of bachelor days. "You know my desire to befriend you is everlasting — that I will never cease, while I know how to do any thing.

But you will always hereafter, be on ground that I have never ocupied, and consequently, if advice were needed, I might advise wrong."

But he "fondly" hoped that Joshua would never again "need any comfort from abroad." If, however, he at times found himself in "the agony of despondency," he must remember he would shortly feel well again. Lincoln had apparently learned that moods tend to go in cycles. "I am now fully convinced, that you love her as ardently as you are capable of loving. Your ever being happy in her presence, and your intense anxiety about her health, if there were nothing else, would place this beyond all dispute in my mind." He advised Joshua to avoid "being *idle*" when he felt depressed; it helped to engage in business and keep busy. Again one feels that Lincoln was tracing the course of his own experience and the methods by which he had worked himself out of his morbid doubts to clear himself of "hypo."

"I hope with tolerable confidence," he continued, "that this letter is a plaster for a place that is no longer sore. God grant it may be so."

Although Lincoln was not yet married, he had insight enough to realize that his letter was not one to be read by Joshua's bride, so he put in a word of caution on that. Recognizing also that he could no longer demand an immediate answer from Joshua the married man, he ended: "Write me whenever you have leisure."

February brought Washington's birthday and in the celebration of it Mr. Lincoln delivered a temperance address in the Second Presbyterian Church. Reading it, one is struck (as so often with Lincoln) by its modern tone. The drunk-ard was not to be treated as "utterly incorrigible" and "damned without remedy," but encouraged to overcome his personal difficulty. Lincoln apparently did not care for the holier-than-thou approach. "In my judgment, such of us as have never fallen victims, have been spared more from the absence of appetite, than from any mental or moral su-periority over those who have."

There is excellent advice on how to win and influence people. "When the conduct of men is designed to be influ-enced, *persuasion*, kind, unassuming persuasion, should ever be adopted. It is an old and true maxim, that a 'drop of honey catches more flies than a gallon of gall.' So with men. If you would win a man to your cause, *first* convince him that you are his sincere friend. Therein is a drop of honey that catches his heart, which, say what he will, is the great high road to his reason. . . ." Do not dictate to or despise the one you wish to win; it is "not much in the nature of man to be driven" to anything.

One finds Lincoln's characteristic device of bringing a point home by a down-to-earth illustration: would the man who said he doubted the power of moral influence or public opinion care "to go to church some Sunday and sit during the sermon with his wife's bonnet upon his head?"

Mary could read that speech three days later in the *San-gamo Journal* and reflect more than ever that she had found her "man of mind," with promise of a future. Knowing her confession that her love remained unchanged and that she missed him, one can imagine the hungry interest with which she read the words that he had spoken. Perhaps as she read she could hear in her mind the tones of the dear, familiar voice.

On the day that the speech appeared in the paper, February 25, Lincoln wrote again to Speed; in fact, in his wisdom, he sent two letters, one for Speed to read by himself and one for him to show his wife. In the letter which was just between the two men, he described the "intense anxiety and trepidation" with which he had opened the first letters received from Joshua after his marriage. Joshua had written that he was still subject to periods of doubt and being miserable, but his friend was sure he saw signs of improvement even in his "*tone* and *handwriting*." "When your nerves once get steady now, the whole trouble will be over forever." Lincoln, who had come out of his mental funk with some good, common-sense, down-to-earth conclusions, summed up matters in one sentence: "I tell you, Speed, our *forebodings,* for which you and I are rather peculiar, are all the worst sort of nonsense."

He continued: ". . . you say you much fear that that Elysium of which you have dreamed so much, is never to be realized." (Decidedly it was wise not to let Fanny read this.) Perhaps the meaning here is that in the mind of every young person there is an ideal picture of what married life should be like, a picture viewed through the bright-colored windows of youth, love, and inexperience which take no account of the adjustments required by the friction of daily existence and by human inability to live forever on the peaks of emotion. Mary had shown something of this innocent viewpoint two years before in her wondering why married folks always become so serious. Lincoln was sure that any such disillusionment would not be the fault of the girl Joshua had married: "I now have no doubt it is the peculiar misfortune of both you and me, to dream dreams of Elysium far exceeding all that any thing earthly can realize. Far short of your dreams as you may be, no woman could do more to realize them, than that same black eyed Fanny."

An enclosed letter was to be shown to Fanny "because, she would think strangely perhaps should you tell her that you receive no letters from me; or, telling her you do, should refuse to let her see them." (Mrs. Edwards had certainly missed it when she said Lincoln was not "intelligent in the female line.") It was a safe letter for Joshua's wife to read, though Lincoln did not conceal his feeling that Joshua's marriage shut out the old intimate relationship between them. "I have no way of telling how much happiness I wish you both; tho' I believe you both can conceive it. I feel som[e]what jealous of both of you now; you will be so exclusively concerned for one another, that I shall be forgotten entirely." He ended by sending Fanny "a double reciprocation of all the love she sent me."

Springfield was all agog again that spring; the magic word "railroad" was being heard on all sides. The first train of the Northern Cross Railroad had run into town on February 15. A wonderful new means of transportation had been built which enabled one to go to Jacksonville on cars that ran on rails and were drawn by engines. What an improvement over the slow-moving stagecoach that mired down in mudholes or overturned in streams! Of course Springfield celebrated this great modern improvement with proper gusto.

A large party of its citizens, accompanied by a stirring band, boarded the short, primitive cars and seated themselves on the benches which ran lengthwise along the sides. With no handholds a sudden jolt was likely to land the passengers in a heap on the floor. Since the little engines burned wood with amazing appetite, the men passengers ran the risk of having to get off and help saw a new supply at the wood stations. Conveniences which one takes for granted now were not even thought of. Yet in that enthusiastic and laughing crowd there were doubtless many who marveled at this modern progress and wondered what would be invented next.

Mary went along with that party on the cars that jolted their way over the bumpy tracks from Springfield to Jacksonville. There they were hospitably received and feasted, for towns as well as their citizens were neighborly. A few weeks later Jacksonville returned the call and was entertained with a sumptuous repast at the American House in Springfield. One likes to imagine the crowds and air of festivity around the square that day.

With her usual joyous responsiveness Molly had a wonderful time on the expedition and word of this came to Lincoln's ears. All he knew of her these days was what mutual friends told him. Molly's enjoyment of the trip was good news to the unselfish man, and about that time he received other good news. His psychiatric patient was getting better.

On March 27 he answered a letter from Joshua: "It can not be told, how it now thrills me with joy, to hear you say

you are *'far happier than you ever expected to be.'* . . . I
say, enough, dear Lord. I am not going beyond the truth,
when I tell you, that the short space it took me to read your
last letter, gave me more pleasure, than the total sum of all
I have enjoyed since that fatal first of Jany. '41." He will
soon be found reasoning from Joshua's story to his own;
perhaps he felt that Joshua's happy ending was a good sign
for him. Self-consciously avoiding the use of her name, just
as she had shied away from using his in her letter to Mercy,
he revealed his thought of Mary as he continued: "Since
then [the fatal first], it seems to me, I should have been entirely happy, but for the never-absent idea, that there is *one*
still unhappy whom I have contributed to make so. That
still kills my soul. I can not but reproach myself, for even
wishing to be happy while she is otherwise. She accompanied a large party on the Rail Road cars, to Jacksonville
last monday; and on her return, spoke, so that I heard of it,
of having enjoyed the trip exceedingly. God be praised for
that."

He told Joshua and Fanny about his temperance speech
and asked them to read it on the ground that "I can not
learn that any body else has read it, or is likely to." Fanny
had enclosed a sweet violet in Joshua's last letter to him. It
was mashed flat, Lincoln said, but he would cherish the
stain which the juice of it had made on the letter "for the
sake of her who procured it. . . ."

How unashamedly sentimental these people were!

CHAPTER 14

"Stand Still and See"

A S spring with its cycle of unfolding leaf and bloom
came to Illinois in 1842, it found Mr. Lincoln in much
healthier mood than that of the year before. Men always
sought his companionship and he was doubtless very good
company when he traveled on the judicial circuit in April
and May. He had nursed Joshua through his emotional crisis to a happy conclusion and perhaps in the process had
come nearer to clarifying his own feelings and situation in
regard to Mary.

It is possible that certain devoted friends were taking
note of the fact that "Richard" was seemingly himself again
and, judging by subsequent events, they decided the time
was ripe to take action in regard to the estranged lovers.

Mary probably wrote almost as many letters as Lincoln
during the first half of that year, but unfortunately none of
them seems to have been preserved. To find out what she
was thinking and doing, the best one can do is to pick up
bits of information about her from the letters of others.
Here that lovely girl, Matilda Edwards, proves helpful
again. In a recently discovered letter which she wrote her
brother Nelson, there is an item which, in consideration of
a certain erroneous idea, is of great importance.

It was in May that Matilda wrote Nelson as follows: "I received a letter from dear Molly this eve pressing me much to visit her. . . ."

Springfield gossip had said that Mr. Lincoln wished to break his engagement with Molly because he had fallen in love with Matilda. If that had been true, Molly, who by her own statement continued to love Mr. Lincoln and stood ready to renew the engagement, would never have invited Matilda to return to Springfield for a visit; the very idea would have sent her into a panic. That should settle for all time the question as to whether Lincoln fell in love with Matilda, but in addition there is her own statement on the subject. Mrs. Edwards once asked her point-blank whether Mr. Lincoln "ever mentioned the subject of his love to her" and the girl answered emphatically: "On my word, he never mentioned such a subject to me: he never even stooped to pay me a compliment."

So at long last it is found that Matilda's name, like that of Sarah Rickard, is a stray thread woven into the tangled knot of the Lincoln love story. When these threads are worked loose from their turns and overlappings, they are found to be detached at each end and not to belong in the knot at all. They were caught into it only by the accident of propinquity.

Lovely, sprightly, conscientious Matilda! Perhaps her brief story should be rounded out too. In the same letter in which she mentioned Molly's invitation for her to visit Springfield (which she declined because "I think I have duties which demand my time at home") she spoke of "Mr S," adding: "I do admire and esteem him very *much*." Gradually one gathers from her letters that her beloved brother Nelson was using his influence in behalf of Mr. Strong's suit, the gentleman being a friend of his and a man of property to boot. One also finds Matilda's resistance to the marriage. In a letter a few months later she states her side of it: "Tis hard, tis hard to school the affections. To admire and love where you are not suited nor destined to love. Indeed it is *impossible*. I may respect, esteem and like but that person is not *the one* to win my love. I would that I were a very different girl."

Mr. Strong, it is interesting to learn from her letters, was also a victim of "hipo." The ailment seemed almost epidemic among gentlemen who were courting. His recital of his gloom bothered Matilda, or, judging by the way she spoke of it, perhaps "bored" would be the better word.

Either she had a change of heart or was finally convinced that it was her duty; at all events she married Newton D. Strong two years later. Her time with him was brief; the family Bible records her death early in 1851 when she was not yet twenty-nine years old. She and Molly remained affectionate friends as long as she lived and Mr. Lincoln was to mention her in terms indicating this friendship in a letter to his wife written when he was in Congress in 1848.

In inviting Matilda to visit her in May 1842, Molly had evidently given the impression that she was very lonesome. But there is further evidence of this fact. Sarah Edwards of Alton did visit Springfield in the late spring of that year and with her help one can cross the little bridge and walk up to the Edwards home on the hill to take a close look at Molly. Sarah found Springfield lacking in its usual gaiety, "but," she wrote, "I spent my time delightfully in a quiet way at home most of the time & when I did not want to see any one of the villagers, would stroll over to Cousin Ninians where it is quite as quiet as any country seat at a distance from town. They see v[ery] little company & since Cousin Elizabeth, united with the church they have given up parties entirely. Molly is as lonesome as a gay company loving, girl, could be so situated. . . ."

Then comes a significant sentence. Sarah, seeing how forlorn the girl was, urged her to come for a visit to Alton but found "we cannot induce her to come down to see us. . . ." Molly made some excuse and Sarah was probably puzzled at her declining the invitation, but Springfield was the place where Mr. Lincoln was and there was the chance that sooner or later she would meet him. Perhaps even then certain events were in the making.

It is worth noting also in Sarah's letter that Elizabeth Edwards, like Matilda, had come to think that parties and dances were inconsistent with religion. Truly she was the last person to understand her gay and sociable sister Molly.

Mr. Lincoln sent another long letter to Joshua early in July. The lawyer had written his friend in April, but the letter dealt mainly with legal and political matters and contained only one item which relates to this story. Lincoln listed the names of the candidates nominated by the Whig county convention and the name of Ninian Edwards was not among them. The letter continued: "Edwards is a little mortified tho' he is quite quiet — and has permitted no one but me to know his feelings. . . ." So the lawyer and Mary's brother-in-law were meeting on good terms in a man's world away from the Edwards home. Mrs. Edwards said her husband opposed the marriage with her, but their son laid the emphasis on his mother's opposition.

Ninian Edwards's attitude toward the Lincoln-Todd wedding is, like his feeling toward Abraham Lincoln through the years, a tangled subject with conflicting evidence. With his mind conditioned by his ideas of aristocracy, Ninian has already been quoted as saying Lincoln was a "mighty Rough man" and "not capable." There is ample evidence, however, that he was friendly toward Lincoln and wanted to help him when he first came to Springfield, even offering to buy him a law library, an offer the newcomer refused, saying he was too poor and did not wish to involve himself.

Opinions and fortunes underwent changes with the years. In the Civil War Edwards lost his prosperity, while Lincoln had become President. Two letters in the Lincoln Papers, both written in 1863, contain some retrospective information about Ninian's position in regard to the marriage. The first of these, which is to Lincoln from William Yates of Springfield, mentioned Ninian Edwards's going to Washington to "*beg*" Lincoln for an appointment. Mr. Yates quoted Ninian as saying ". . . that you must do something for him, that he had greatly befriended you, when you were poor and unknown. Had helped you to get your wife & that unless you did, He would [be] ruined."

The second, a long letter from Ninian himself to Lincoln, is in the same vein. Ninian reminded Lincoln of his "*devoted attachment*" to him in early days. "I would like to ask you," continued this letter, "if when you were a young man I was not your most devoted friend in more ways than one. Let . . . your own recollection, and a letter of yours written to me in 1842 before your marriage answer." The mention of this letter of Lincoln's to Ninian at such a time is almost unbearably intriguing, yet this reference to it is all one has today.

Lincoln's telling Joshua in 1842 that Ninian permitted no one but himself to know he was mortified indicates a close degree of friendship that year. It is possible Ninian had become reconciled to the marriage and that he did assist "in more ways than one." It should be taken into account, however, that Ninian desperately wanted Lincoln's help when he expressed such devoted attachment to him in 1863.

In Lincoln's letter to Joshua in July one learns that their roles have been reversed: Joshua was now advising Lincoln about his state of mind and love tangle. Lincoln replied that the subject was painful to him and nothing could make him forget it. "I acknowledge the correctness of your advice too; but before I resolve to do the one thing or the other, I must regain my confidence in my own ability to keep my resolves when they are made. In that ability, you know, I once prided myself as the only, or at least the chief, gem of my character; that gem I lost — how, and when, you too well know." He had not yet regained it and until he did, he could not trust himself in any matter of much importance. "I believe now that, had you understood my case at the time, as well as I understood yours afterwards, by the aid you would have given me, I should have sailed through clear; but that does not now afford me sufficient confidence, to begin that, or the like of that, again." If one only knew what Joshua had advised!

Joshua had expressed in his letter his obligations to his friend for helping him achieve his "present happiness." Lincoln was greatly pleased with this acknowledgment, "but a thousand times more am I pleased to know, that you enjoy a degree of happiness, worthy of an acknowledgement."

Then comes one of the most significant passages in all the letters to Joshua, a passage which brings into focus both the stage at which Lincoln had arrived in his long-drawn-out mental conflict and the nature of his religious feeling. He explained to Joshua that in advising him he felt he was being used by the divine will: "The truth is, I am not sure there was any merit, with me, in the part I took in your difficulty; I was drawn to it as by fate; if I would, I could not have done less than I did. I always was superstitious; and as part of my superstition, I believe God made me one of the instruments of bringing your Fanny and you together, which union, I have no doubt He had fore-ordained." A new note follows, an uplift of spirit, of hope for himself. "Whatever he designs, he will do for *me* yet. 'Stand *still* and see the salvation of the Lord' is my text just now."

It often happens that people who have come through a long, baffling, exhausting siege of the spirit, grappling with problems that seem to have no solution, unable to decide which course of action to take, cease struggling to turn to their religious faith and rest their weary souls in waiting for a revelation of divine guidance. Such was Lincoln's state now. He was a man of deep religious feeling. All the rest of his life one finds incidents in which he placed his reliance on the will of God. In the dark days of the Civil War Presidency, at a meeting of his Cabinet in the fall of 1862, he was to say to that grave and troubled circle of men: "When the rebel army was at Frederick, I determined, as soon as it should be driven out of Maryland, to issue a Proclamation of Emancipation. . . . I said nothing to anyone; but I made the promise to myself, and (hesitating a little) — to my Maker. The rebel army is now driven out, and I am going to fulfill that promise." He was to say simply at the perplexing and tragic time when he was re-elected for the second term: "I will put my trust in God."

Just as he had asked a sign of the divine will in regard to the Emancipation Proclamation, he was, early in July 1842, waiting for Providence to indicate what he should do about his love affair and whether his union with Mary Todd also was "fore-ordained." Providence was to give him an unmistakable answer very shortly; it is possible that its chosen "instruments" had already made their warmhearted little plot.

It had been a year and a half now since the engagement had been broken, eighteen sad and perplexed months. In them Lincoln had learned a great deal. He had not been able to get Mary out of his mind. The thought that she was unhappy killed his very soul. He had written to Joshua in his newly acquired wisdom that one does not reason himself into falling in love, neither is one able to reason oneself out of it. He had found out in misery and loneliness that one great test of love is whether one is happy in the presence of the beloved and always anxious about her wellbeing. He had expressed to Joshua his belief that it is possible for a man to have grave doubts as to his love for a girl and still love her as ardently as he is capable of loving. He had emerged from his dark questionings and fears into the healthy conclusion that his peculiar forebodings were "all the worst sort of nonsense."

Mr. Lincoln had apparently not seen Mary during those months. He could not go to the Edwards home and he had avoided gatherings which she was likely to attend. Mary, as a restricted Victorian female, was not apt to frequent the common haunts of men. And Mr. Lincoln was away from Springfield a great deal of the time on the judicial circuit. Perhaps at times she had seen a tall, thin figure on the streets of Springfield, a distant glimpse that stirred deep longing; perhaps similarly Mr. Lincoln had caught sight of a girlish form with the result that his sensitive face had become charged with emotion. One wonders whether there were not times at night when he walked southwest through the dark streets in the direction of the little bridge and looked up the hill to the big house where an upstairs window was dimly outlined by candlelight. Did he picture Molly behind that square of light and wonder whether her face was gay and happy, as he had loved to see it, or stained with tears as on that fatal New Year's Day?

In the minds of each of them was the image of the other bound up with the memories of a time of happiness and affection followed by a long-drawn-out desolation.

It might have been predicted that friends would try to bring them together again. All the world delights to help lovers in distress; it is a nice human trait. Here were two popular, fine young people who inspired devoted friendship in others and both were dissatisfied and lonely. It was a state of affairs that any warmhearted, motherly woman with a normal feminine instinct for matchmaking would find impossible to resist. Such a woman was Mrs. Simeon Francis, wife of the publisher of the *Sangamo Journal*, who was devoted to Lincoln. Mrs. Francis was a warm friend of Mary Todd's. It is recorded that Dr. Henry also had part in bringing the lovers together; perhaps he knew what was going to happen at the Simeon Francis home.

The details of the little conspiracy, whether Mr. Lincoln was asked casually to drop in at that home at a certain day and hour or how the coming of Mary was arranged, are not known. One only knows that the tall lawyer unexpectedly found himself in a room with a girl whose bright chestnut head would scarcely come to his shoulder, a girl who lifted startled blue eyes to meet his own. Mrs. Francis had succeeded at last in bringing Mary Todd and Abraham Lincoln face to face without either having warning of what was to happen. Sympathetically and simply she told them to be friends again.

Providence had pointed the way to Mr. Lincoln with a vengeance.

CHAPTER 15

Secret Meetings

THERE is no record of the details of that meeting. One can only imagine Mary's questioning and hungry searching of Mr. Lincoln's rugged face, noting perhaps that it appeared a little more lined than she remembered it. It may have seemed more dear to her on account of this. That face must have pictured deep emotion as he looked down at the fresh prettiness of the girl whose color and aliveness made any mental image of her seem pale by comparison. What are remembered impressions against the warm vital surge of attraction between two young people who love each other and meet again after a long desolate separation?

The first difficult and halting words that each said at that meeting cannot now be recovered; but the result is known. With the devoted encouragement of Mr. and Mrs. Simeon Francis, it was arranged that the two should continue to have secret meetings at the Francis home. Elizabeth Edwards, trying in every possible way to prevent a marriage between her sister Mary and Mr. Lincoln, must know nothing of what was going on. There was an additional motive for concealment. When two people have had a broken engagement involving deep emotions and that very private matter has become the talk of the town, they naturally want to keep the renewal of their attachment hidden until they are sure of themselves. When Mrs. Edwards finally did find out about the meetings (after it was too late for her to interfere), Mary explained to her "that the world — woman & man were uncertain & slippery and that it was best to keep the secret courtship from all eyes & ears."

A new period now began, a time of delightful plotting for these stolen visits together when the tall lawyer could again glue his eyes on the glowing face of Mary, when they could laugh and talk, and indulge in repartee and whimsical make-believe as they had in the golden days when they were falling in love and were first engaged. To use the pleasant little name "Molly" was again easy and natural to Mr. Lincoln; there was no more constrained reference to her as "*one* still unhappy."

But both had gained in maturity in the many months of separation. They had pondered the serious questions of marriage in general and between themselves in particular. Mary, against the barrage of family advice as to the mistake of taking a husband who lacked family background and early education, in short the mistake of marrying beneath her, had never wavered in her love for and confidence in Mr. Lincoln. She had found her man of talent with what she, in spite of belittling comments by relatives, considered a bright future.

She had come through the long ordeal with more poise than he had. Later in their lives these roles would be reversed, she would be the one who suffered from emotional instability and he would be the one to keep his balance. She would then lean on his strength. The sensitiveness and the understanding of a nervous temperament which he had re-vealed in his letters to Joshua would stand him in good stead in his marriage to a nervous, excitable girl.

Mr. Lincoln's whole life was a process of growth and de-velopment. This was especially true of the hard period through which he had just passed. He had undergone great humiliation and emerged from it with added strength. (An-other supremely humiliating experience was just ahead of him, but he could not foresee that.) He had had lessons in self-discipline, had learned to reason himself out of the dark moods with which he would always have to struggle. He had developed in his religious faith. He had learned earlier perhaps than most that there are times to stand still and await the revelation of divine will.

One wonders whether Mrs. Edwards noticed that Mary's spirits were better and that she no longer wore the forlorn aspect noted by the visiting cousin, Sarah Edwards. The secret of the meetings with Mr. Lincoln seems to have been well kept from Mary's sister, though necessarily a few intimate friends knew of them. With such things as tele-phones undreamed of, the lovers had to have go-betweens who would carry notes and messages back and forth. Dr. Henry may well have served in this way as he could see both Mary and Mr. Lincoln without any suspicions being aroused. At least it is said that he helped the reconciliation along in some way and the Lincolns always loved him. The time was to come in the far future when he would visit the White House and in the quick emotion of old friendship re-newed would impulsively greet the First Lady with a kiss.

It is also part of the record that one of Mary's friends,

Julia Jayne, was in the secret and was sometimes present in the little group at the Francis home.

One cannot tell exactly when the engagement was renewed. But with Mr. Lincoln following the direction indicated by Providence, and continuing to meet Mary again and again, one does not need the wisdom of Providence to know that a renewed engagement was a foregone conclusion. The basic fact was that these two genuinely loved each other and all that was needed was the opportunity to meet.

Mary with her love of drama undoubtedly got many thrills from the whole intriguing situation and delighted in every detail connected with arranging the secret meetings. No longer were the days to her "flat, stale & unprofitable" and "of *interminable* length"; they were highlighted by those precious rendezvous. Mr. Lincoln was his old self again, in happy spirits and the best of company. What had he said about the test of love being happiness in the presence of the loved one? Some of those dark problems which had weighed him down had dissolved; others were dissolving in the satisfaction of being with Molly again. They had gaiety and laughter with those wonderful friends Mr. and Mrs. Francis and with the few others who were in the delightful secret.

There were two most important topics discussed at those stolen meetings — love and politics. The first will be left exclusively to Abraham and Mary, but the second involved Mr. Francis, editor of that staunchly Whig newspaper the *Sangamo Journal,* and a certain sniping conflict between Whigs and Democrats late that summer. This love story, as has been seen, was destined to be entangled with politics in an amazing fashion. Having brought the lovers together, fate was preparing for them a most dramatic and fearful surprise. Both of them were to act impulsively and with a lack of balanced consideration and to face, as a result, some startling consequences.

It must be remembered that, following the panic of 1837, the year 1842 was one of financial difficulty. Hard times were contributing much to the prevailing "hypo." The state banks at Springfield and Shawneetown both failed and their notes were passing at large discounts. The State of Illinois did not want its taxes paid in these depreciated bank notes and the people had practically nothing else with which to pay them. Nearly all good money had been driven out of the state.

To protect its government from loss the state auditor issued a proclamation ordering collectors to suspend the collection of revenue and not, under any conditions, to accept state bank paper at more than its current, depreciated value. The state auditor happened to be that striking Irishman James Shields, already introduced as a member of the coterie. Being a Democrat, he was a political opponent of Lincoln, Simeon Francis, and other Whigs. People were dismayed at the proclamation which put them in an almost impossible position in regard to their taxes and Mr. Shields, though his action was justified in itself, was being bombarded with unfavorable comment.

The Whigs, of course, seized the chance to make political thunder and tear down a prominent Democrat. Mr. Shields was an especially choice target because his over-elaborate manners made him a bit pompous and because he took himself so seriously. There was undoubtedly much talk of this action of Mr. Shields's at the gatherings at the Francis home and, one suspects, much jesting and laughter at the Irishman's foibles. Imagination even pictures Mary, with her flare for mimicry, giving a lively imitation of his elaborate gallantry. Apparently there was generated at those meetings a contagious spirit of making fun of Mr. Shields.

Not long before this, Mr. Francis's newspaper, the *Sangamo Journal*, had printed an anonymous letter which purported to come from "Rebecca," an appealingly countrified woman who lived in the "Lost Townships." "Rebecca" discussed current questions in humorous backwoods dialect, the letter thus serving as an engaging way of getting certain ideas across. It has been suggested that this letter was written by Simeon Francis. But shortly after Shields's unpopular proclamation, Mr. Lincoln seized on this device, probably after a chuckling conference with Simeon, to present some Whig remarks on the state tax question with much humorous lampooning of Mr. Shields. Subsequent events suggest that Mary too was in this scheme to poke fun at the state auditor. It is quite possible the whole thing was laughingly planned at one of the meetings at the Francis home. At all events, Lincoln wrote a letter signed "Rebecca" and headed "Lost Townships" which was published in the *Sangamo Journal* on September 2.

Reading it one is assured that Mr. Lincoln was in fine fettle and brimming over with twinkling humor. Backwoods dialect was no problem to him — he had grown up with it

— his problem had been to get rid of it. "Rebecca" tells how, after cleaning up the dinner dishes, she stepped over to the cabin of her neighbor, Jeff, "to see if his wife Peggy was as well as mought be expected, and hear what they called the baby." When she got there, she found Jeff "setting on the door-step reading a newspaper."

In the words of "Rebecca's" letter: " 'How are you Jeff,' says I, — he sorter started when he heard me, for he hadn't seen me before. 'Why,' says he, 'I'm mad as the devil, aunt Becca.'

" 'What about,' says I, 'aint its hair the right color? None of that nonsense, Jeff — there aint an honester woman in the Lost Township than — '

" 'Than who? ' says he, 'what the mischief are you about?'

"I began to see I was running the wrong trail, and so says I, 'O nothing, I guess I was mistaken a little, that's all. But what is it you're mad about?' "

What Jeff was mad about was what a great many other people were mad about, the fact that he had worked very hard "to raise State Bank paper enough" to pay his taxes and now he had just read in the paper that tax collectors were forbidden "to receive State paper at all." If he sold "all the plunder" he had, he still would not have enough cash to pay his taxes.

Aunt Becca was much startled at this news herself, but the chance for an argument was too good to be missed: "I saw Jeff was in a good tune for saying some ill-natured things, and so I tho't I would just argue a little on the contrary side, and make him rant a spell if I could."

With the aid of a little profanity Jeff presented his arguments and then the two, examining the newspaper again, found that the author of the proclamation was James Shields. Jeff, of course, disagreed violently with Shields's statement of the object of the measure. " 'I say its a lie, and not a well told one at that. It grins out like a copper dollar. Shields is a fool as well as a liar. With him truth is out of the question, and as for getting a good bright passable lie out of him, you might as well try to strike fire from a cake of tallow. I stick to it, its all an infernal whig lie.' "

Jeff, of course, was a Democrat but had no intention of admitting that Shields was one too. Aunt Becca, being a Whig herself, at once challenged him as to calling Shields a Whig. Jeff stood his ground: " 'I tell you, aunt Becca, there's no mistake about his being a whig — why his very looks shows it — every thing about him shows it — if I was deaf and blind I could tell him by the smell.' " One can almost see the deepening twinkle in Lincoln's eyes as his pen continued with Jeff's words: " 'I seed him [Shields] when I was down in Springfield last winter. They had a sort of gatherin there one night, among the grandees, they called a fair. All the galls [gals] about town was there, and all the handsome widows, and married women, finickin about, trying to look like galls, tied as tight in the middle, and puffed out at both ends like bundles of fodder that hadn't been stacked yet, but wanted stackin pretty bad.' "

Jeff described the fair: " 'And then they had tables all round the house kivered over with baby caps, and pin-cushions, and ten thousand such little nicknacks, tryin to sell 'em to the fellows that were bowin and scrapin, and kun-

geerin about 'em.' " Among these attentive gentlemen was
" 'this same fellow Shields floatin about on the air, without
heft or earthly substance, just like a lock of cat-fur where
cats had been fightin . . . his very features, in the ex-
static agony of his soul, spoke audibly and distinctly —
"Dear girls, *it is distressing*, but I cannot marry you all. Too
well I know how much you suffer; but do, *do* remember, it
is not my fault that I am *so* handsome and *so* interesting." ' "
Jeff clinched his argument: " 'He a democrat! Fiddle-sticks!
I tell you, aunt Becca, he's a whig, and no mistake: nobody
but a whig could make such a conceity dunce of himself.' "

It was all very clever and funny but not exactly the thing
to say about a fighting Irishman, especially one who had
been trained in swordplay. If, as suspected, the letter had
been discussed in one of those hilarious meetings at the
Francis home when Mary, Mr. Lincoln, and Simeon Francis were all present and one mirthful sally led to another,
the possible reaction of Mr. Shields had not been considered as carefully as it should have been.

But writing humorous anonymous letters to ridicule a political foe was apparently lots of fun. In the next step Mary
decided to try her hand at a "Rebecca" letter. She and her
friend Julia Jayne put their heads together and, doubtless
with many girlish giggles, concocted another letter in the
same vein which was published in the *Sangamo Journal* on
September 9. One learns from it without surprise that Mr.
Shields had not liked the "Rebecca" letter written by Mr.
Lincoln: ". . . the man what Jeff seed down to the fair"
was "threatnin' to take personal satisfaction of the writer."
In Mary's and Julia's letter, "Rebecca" says that when she

heard this, "I was so skart that I tho't I should quill-wheel right where I was."

She is ready to make apology rather than fight and first offers Mr. Shields the "satisfaction" of squeezing her hand. "If that ain't personal satisfaction, I can only say that he is the fust man that was not satisfied with squeezin' my hand." But if Mr. Shields still wants to fight, rather than "get a lickin" she, being a widow, offers to marry him. "I know he's a fightin' man, and would rather fight than eat; but isn't marryin' better than fightin', though it does sometimes run into it? And I don't think, upon the whole, that I'd be sich a bad match neither — I'm not over sixty, and am just four feet three in my bare feet, and not much more around the girth. . . ."

If, however, Mr. Shields insists on fighting: "Jeff tells me the way these fire-eaters do is to give the challenged party choice of weapons, etc., which bein' the case, I'll tell you in confidence that I never fights with anything but broomsticks or hot water or a shovelful of coals or some such thing. . . . I will give him choice, however, in one thing, and that is, whether, when we fight, I shall wear breeches or he petticoats, for, I presume that change is sufficient to place us on an equality." The two girls were rather letting their instinct for funmaking run away with them. Molly characteristically was plunging into action that she would later regret.

At this point in the love story of Abraham and Mary there appears a strange and quaint document which is now a collector's item. It is a prosaic document on the face of it,

yet it is laced with pink ribbon and stirs the imagination in
its sentimental meaning. In Lincoln's own handwriting,
which is larger than usual, is a list of all candidates for the
state legislature from the time he first ran until his last can-
didacy, with the number of votes for each. Examining it,
one finds a striking demonstration of his increasing political
strength and popularity; he rises from a vote of something
over six hundred in 1832 to the very top of the list with a
vote of more than seventeen hundred in 1836. He had prepared this list, playfully had it certified by his friend
N. W. Matheny, the county clerk, tied it with pink ribbon,
and presented it to Mary on the very day her "Rebecca" letter appeared in the *Sangamo Journal*. The cautious bachelor
had come a long way by this time; he was evidently proving to his girl that he was an increasingly important man politically. But she did not need this gay, whimsical, lawyerlike proving; her faith in him was always to be boundless.
That Mary kept and treasured this sentimental document
is made clear by the fact that it exists today, an appealing
bit of evidence of the fun, banter, and lovemaking that was
going on at those secret meetings of the lovers in the Francis home.

CHAPTER 16

Challenged to a Duel

A S Mary remembered it years later, she and Mr. Lincoln were engaged again by the time of the "Rebecca" letters. With these meetings going on and a number of people necessarily knowing about them, rumors were floating around connecting their names. She was carrying off her part beautifully and doubtless enjoying it tremendously, now that all was well between her and her lover. A relative, speaking later of this period, told how other girls, perhaps hoping to get some information on the subject, tried to tease her about her "tall beau." (That adjective certainly identified him, as both Mr. Douglas and Mr. Webb were decidedly of the short variety.) Mary "bore their jokes and teasings good naturedly but would give them no satisfaction, neither affirming nor denying the report of her engagement to Mr. Lincoln." It will be seen that sister Elizabeth was unaware of what was brewing.

Mary was acting with unusual discretion in keeping her secret, but she was about to make a move she would later regret. Writing an anonymous piece to appear in a Springfield paper where it would be read by all her friends was so exhilarating that she had another bright idea. She would do a poem on Mr. Shields. She would pretend that he had accepted that ridiculous marriage proposal by "Rebecca" which she and Julia Jayne had impudently put into their letter. Since she wanted to use "Rebecca" in the third person, she signed this effusion "Cathleen."

One can imagine the red-faced indignation of Mr. Shields (who had already been brought to the boiling point) when he read in the *Sangamo Journal* on September 16:

> Ye jews-harps awake! The [Auditor]'s won —
> Rebecca the widow has gained Erin's son;
> The pride of the north from the Emerald isle
> Has been woo'd and won by a woman's sweet smile.
> The combat's relinquished, old loves all forgot:
> To the widow he's bound, Oh! bright be his lot!

Marrying Mr. Shields to the short, stout, elderly, countrified "Rebecca" was insult enough, but the verses also paid their respects to his excessive gallantry, a theme Lincoln had treated so devastatingly in his "Rebecca" letter.

> Happy groom! in sadness far distant from thee
> The FAIR girls dream only of past times of glee
> Enjoyed in thy presence; whilst the *soft blarnied store*
> Will be fondly remembered as relics of yore,
> And hands that in rapture you oft would have prest,
> In prayer will be clasp'd that your lot may be blest.

Mary confessed years later that she wrote these lines, adding with the perspective (and regret) which time had brought: ". . . and very silly verses they were . . . said to abound in sarcasm, causing them to be very offensive" to Mr. Shields. One suspects the jingle had been the subject of animated discussion and laughter at one of the meetings in the Francis home, as her account continued: "A gentleman friend, carried them off, and . . . one day, I saw them, strangely enough in the daily papers." The gentleman friend presumably was Simeon Francis, editor of the *Sangamo Journal*.

At some point the infuriated Shields communicated with Mr. Francis and demanded the name of the person who was writing these insulting contributions. As Mary understood it, Simeon asked for a short delay and in that interval got in touch with Mr. Lincoln, who had written only the one letter published on September 2. The lawyer at once replied: ". . . say to Shields, that 'I am responsible.' " He thereby took the blame for what Mary had written as well as for his own letter.

The day "Cathleen's" effusion appeared Mr. Shields went into action. The only reason he had not done so sooner, as he took care to explain, was that he had been unavoidably absent from Springfield on public business. Now, sizzling with the additional insult of the verses, he could hardly wait to settle accounts with Mr. Lincoln. Learning that the lawyer was at Tremont, Illinois, about sixty-five miles from Springfield, attending court, and that he was likely to be out on the judicial circuit for several weeks, Mr. Shields, with his friend General John D. Whiteside (who would act as his second, if necessary), started to that town to catch up with Lincoln. Trained in fencing and swordplay, the auditor was thinking in terms of a duel.

The startling news of Shields's departure and intentions quickly reached those devoted friends of Mr. Lincoln's, William Butler and Dr. Merryman. They departed posthaste for Tremont, hoping to reach Mr. Lincoln before

Shields arrived, warn him, and offer their assistance. They did not trust him to know the "diplomacy" of dueling as they did, though judging by subsequent events, diplomacy was the last word one would associate with these two hotheads. They seemed more concerned that negotiations should be conducted according to the "code duello" than with any desire to avoid the fight itself.

Apparently they traveled on horseback. According to Dr. Merryman, he and Butler followed Shields and Whiteside so quickly that they were able to pass them during the night and get to Mr. Lincoln first. There was exciting drama in that night journey, with the rapid hoofbeats on the dark road that carried the menacing news nearer and nearer to the unsuspecting Mr. Lincoln asleep at Tremont. He had not realized that the funmaking had gotten so out of hand. One can imagine his grave face and whirling thoughts when his friends revealed to him he was facing the prospect of a duel with Shields. He told them, related Dr. Merryman, that he was completely opposed to the practice of dueling and would do anything to avoid it that would not lower him in his own estimation and that of his friends, but he would fight rather than be thus degraded.

Shields opened negotiations with the stiff formal note of a man accustomed to the dueling code. It was written on Saturday, September 17, at Tremont and was properly delivered to Mr. Lincoln by Shields's representative, General Whiteside. The auditor informed "A. Lincoln, Esq." (without salutation) that he regretted "the disagreeable nature" of his communication; he had, he said, endeavored "to conduct myself in such a way amongst both my political friends and opponents" as to "avoid any difficulty with any one in Springfield. . . ." But "whilst thus abstaining from giving provocation, I have become the object of slander, vituperation and personal abuse, which were I capable of submitting to, I would prove myself worthy of the whole of it."

Referring to the objectionable articles in the *Sangamo Journal,* he continued: "On enquiring I was informed by the editor of that paper . . . that you are the author of those articles. . . . I will take the liberty of requiring a full, positive and absolute retraction of all offensive allusions used by you in these communications, in relation to my private character and standing as a man, as an apology for the insults conveyed in them."

The letter ended on an ominous note: "This may prevent consequences which no one will regret more than myself." He was "Your ob't serv't, Jas. Shields."

It is possible that if the tactful Mr. Lincoln, who deeply regretted the length to which the matter had gone and who had no real enmity toward Mr. Shields, could have talked to him directly and told him these things, the quarrel would have been patched up then and there. But negotiations had to go through the zealous friends who were determined that this affair of honor should be properly conducted, no matter who got killed. And it is also true that at this time Mr. Lincoln himself had a very sensitive dignity. At all events, and perhaps after a stiffening conference with Dr. Merryman and Mr. Butler, he answered Mr. Shields's note on that very Saturday in much the same tone the auditor had used.

As to the articles in the paper, wrote Mr. Lincoln, ". . . without stopping to enquire whether I really am the author, or to point out what is offensive in them, you demand an unqualified retraction of all that is offensive; and then proceed to hint at consequences."

His phrasing was as stiff-necked as Shields's as he continued: "Now, sir, there is in this so much assumption of facts, and so much of menace as to consequences, that I cannot submit to answer that note any farther than I have, and to add, that the consequence to which I suppose you allude, would be a matter of as great regret to me as it possibly could to you." He was "Respectfully, A. Lincoln."

There was still time on that crowded Saturday at Tremont for Mr. Shields to write another note. In this he asked Mr. Lincoln the direct question whether he was the author of the "Rebecca" letter which had appeared on September 2 (which of course he was) or any other article over the same signature. If Mr. Lincoln had not written any of these contributions, his denial would be sufficient, but if he had, Mr. Shields repeated his "request of an absolute retraction of all offensive allusion contained therein. . . ."

This was not delivered to Mr. Lincoln that day. According to Dr. Merryman's account, General Whiteside conferred with William Butler, who told him that Mr. Lincoln could not receive any communication from Mr. Shields unless it were a withdrawal of his first note or a challenge to a duel. However, on the following Monday General Whiteside delivered this same note to Mr. Lincoln, who read it and returned it to the General saying he did not think it consistent with his honor to negotiate for peace with Mr. Shields unless he would withdraw his former offensive letter.

The next step was that Mr. Shields notified Mr. Lincoln that General Whiteside was to be his second. Mr. Lincoln at once answered designating Dr. Merryman as his. The duel was on. The two seconds then had a conference to see whether they could patch up the quarrel, though Whiteside declared that if Shields knew of this attempt on his part to restore peace without fighting, the overwrought Irishman would be apt to challenge him next or would as soon cut his throat as not.

Mr. Lincoln was in a most harrowing position. All his sense of justice and humanitarianism was revolted by the brutal practice of dueling, which in some cases amounted to murder with due ceremony. He could have had little taste for the elaborate etiquette and ritual by which the deadly combat was conducted. But there was no cowardice in this man; it was not his nature to dodge an issue or a fight where either should be squarely met. When he had been living in New Salem, he had engaged in rough wrestling matches with a certain good-natured gusto. But duels were a matter of pistols or the cold steel of swords, of wounds and bleeding and, too often, death. Nevertheless, his fighting blood and a certain stubborn resistance were aroused. He was once more in a position which left no completely satisfactory course of action open to him, but he would fight.

How could he do otherwise? There was a special angle to his situation. Only a "gentleman" could fight a duel; it was a method of settling disputes between "gentlemen," not used by the lower classes. By the "code duello," if a man refused a challenge, he was considered a coward and not a gentleman. Lincoln was having to do his courting secretly at this time because Mary's relatives regarded him as on a lower social level. It seemed as if they did not consider that he had the standing of a gentleman. If he failed to accept Shields's challenge, he would expose himself to their ridicule as well as the scorn of political opponents and all who accepted the usual ideas associated with dueling. He had said he would not submit to "such degradation." It would have injured him gravely in the fields of both love and politics.

He could not let Mary down. He had assumed responsibility for what she had done. In a contagious spirit of fun the lighthearted girl had gone further than she should have. But so had he and he had started the whole thing. There was an unhappy train of thought in that direction too. Upon sober reflection, away from the stimulation of a fun-loving little group, this thing of writing anonymous letters in order to ridicule did not seem exactly a fair or right-minded thing to do.

Lincoln had missed more than book training in his early years in a rude environment; he had missed learning certain intangible standards of a cultured society. In many respects he had had no chance to learn "how to behave." Anonymous ridicule had been considered "smart" among the log-cabin folk with whom he had lived in his teens back in Indiana. At twenty he had written anonymously "The Chronicles of Reuben," a strongly flavored narrative making fun of two sons of the Grigsby family into which his sister Sarah had married. It had circulated briskly and made a tremendous hit among his unlettered neighbors, whose collective sense of humor was constructed on robust lines, and he had doubtless received many a hearty backslapping of approbation. But heaven knew he had provocation enough in that case, knew what bitterness lay back of that biting ridicule, remembering that the Grigsbys had not been good to Sarah and she had died in childbirth as the result, he thought, of their neglect. One is not apt to care how rough the weapon when one is striking back for a hurt like that.

But Mr. Shields was an honorable man who had merely done his public duty and had been subjected to a cruel belittling in regard to it. He had no way of restoring his dignity except by the challenge to a duel according to the code by which he had been trained. Mr. Lincoln's sensitive conscience was to hurt him; never again would he stoop to use anonymous ridicule. He had learned out of humiliating experience to restrain his great and devastating gift of wit and mimicry while he considered its effect upon its human target. It was not the mature Lincoln who wrote that anonymous letter but a Mr. Lincoln who was still growing up. The courtship period usually furnishes a liberal education for any man, but he was getting all the required courses plus some extra ones.

CHAPTER 17

Bloody Island

MR. Lincoln and Dr. Merryman returned to Springfield from Tremont by buggy, arriving late Monday night after a long, tiring journey. They found the town in a fever of excitement over the proposed duel. One can imagine the agitated little groups of men that gathered around the square to discuss the matter, the flushed faces and anxious eyes of Mr. Lincoln's friends, the violent disagreements over a situation which originated in the antagonism between the two political parties. Dueling itself in Illinois was startling enough and certainly no one would expect Springfield, politically red-hot as it was, to be calm over a duel where one principal was a leading — and popular — Whig and the other a prominent Democrat. The town had not been so aroused since the murder mystery.

And murder this might well turn out to be. One can almost hear the people talking. Mr. Shields was trained in the art of dueling, but who could imagine Mr. Lincoln with a sword or pistol in hand? He was a good wrestler and could hold his own in a rough and tumble fight, which was the good old American way of settling a quarrel around these parts. But what chance had that slow, awkward figure of a man against the skill and agility of a trained duelist? And didn't they know dueling in Illinois was a penitentiary offense? Mr. Lincoln was sure to be arrested. And Mr. Shields and General Whiteside had better look out too, or they would lose their important jobs, because a man could be deprived of the right to hold public office and subjected to a big fine for even sending a challenge or acting as a second in a duel. So, one imagines, ran the comments on the streets and in the homes of Springfield.

The coterie, to which the principals both belonged, was in a dither. One can picture the apprehensive faces of James and Mercy Conkling, of Julia Jayne, who had had a part in one of the "Rebecca" letters, of all to whom the personalities of Mr. Shields and Mr. Lincoln were so familiar. One can also imagine the Edwards-Todd group of relatives remarking that it was just like Mr. Lincoln to get himself into a scrape like that. They probably knew nothing of Mary's part in the anonymous publications or that he had taken the responsibility for what she had done.

And what were the thoughts and emotions of the girl who loved Mr. Lincoln and was partly responsible for getting him into this situation? Years later she wrote her full account of the dueling incident and revealed in so doing her tender pride at his protection of her and her regret for her own thoughtlessness. Like girls in general and especially like the girls of that sentimental era, she loved the romantic and dramatic and delighted in stories of the age of chivalry. (She would one day read those stirring tales to her little sons.) She thought of Mr. Lincoln as her gallant knight, "my champion," as she proudly wrote it, and the chivalry of his championship remained precious to her through all the years.

But along with her loving pride at this tense moment went remorse and fear. She was always one to acknowledge her faults in the end and, writing of this period later and mentioning Mr. Lincoln's devotion to her, she said contritely: "I doubtless trespassed, many times & oft, upon his great tenderness & amiability of character." Added to this was fear for the man whose life was always to be dearer to her than her own.

She had learned full well about duels back home among the hotheaded Kentuckians. The year before she came to Springfield to live, a political duel had involved three of her father's intimate friends and resulted in the death of one of the parties. She could remember the furor about it, and the horror of the tragedy. She doubtless knew also that Mr. Shields was a skilled swordsman. In the Edwards home on the hill Mary's head must have tossed feverishly on her pillow that night of Monday, September 19, and one doubts whether Mr. Lincoln ever got to bed at all at the Butler home.

He, an upright lawyer of the town, was in danger of arrest for violation of the law. He would have to leave Springfield immediately. But first he must write out instructions for Dr. Merryman, who would represent him. (As a matter of fact, Dr. Merryman was violating the law also in acting as go-between for a duel and would shortly have to leave town himself.)

One can read today Lincoln's instructions, which were perhaps drawn up in the dark hours of that Monday night. He first told Dr. Merryman to offer a full apology to Shields if the auditor would withdraw his first note and

substitute another which was "without menace, or dicta-
tion." If Shields did this and asked without offense whether
Lincoln was the author of the articles, Merryman was to
read him Lincoln's answer: "I did write the 'Lost Township' letter which appeared in the Journal of the 2nd Inst.
but had no participation, in any form, in any other article
alluding to you." Lincoln continued that he wrote the letter "wholly for political effect," that he had no intention of
injuring Shields's standing as a gentleman, and that he did
not think the letter had produced that effect. If he had anticipated such an effect, he said, "I would have forborne to
write it. And I will add, that your conduct towards me, so
far as I knew, had always been gentlemanly; and that I had
no personal pique against you, and no cause for any."

If, however, Shields would not withdraw his first note,
the lawyer gave Dr. Merryman instructions for the duel itself. Fortunately Lincoln, as the challenged party, had the
choice of weapons. One has to smile a little over the shrewdness of his selection and at the conditions he specified for
the duel, if duel there must be. The weapons were to be
"Cavalry broad swords of the largest size, precisely equal
in all respects." Such an enormous sword plus Lincoln's
height and almost abnormal length of arm would add up to
a reach that Shields, a shorter man, could not possibly
achieve.

To make this reach an advantage, however, there had to
be something to prevent Shields from getting too close to
Lincoln. The conditions specified that a certain space was
to be set off for the duel and in the middle of this space a
plank was to be set on edge in the ground "as the line be-

tween us which neither is to pass his foot over upon forfeit of his life." As Lincoln said later, he did not want to kill Shields and believed that he, having practiced somewhat with the broadsword, could disarm him, but he added: "I didn't want the d——d fellow to kill me, which I rather think he would have done if we had selected pistols."

Mr. Lincoln left Springfield early Tuesday morning and went to Jacksonville, where, one suspects, he put in a good deal of time at broadsword practice. It brings a strangely un-Lincolnian picture to mind to think of that tall, angular figure with enormous sword in hand going through the motions and learning the technique of sword fighting.

It is not necessary to follow the ins and outs of the various meetings and arrangements between the two seconds, Dr. Merryman and General Whiteside. Both by this time wanted to settle the quarrel without the fight, but one trouble was that Whiteside hesitated even to make a pacific suggestion to the infuriated auditor; he would as soon think of asking Shields to butt his brains out against a brick wall as to ask him to withdraw his first note. And withdrawing that first note was the only condition under which Lincoln would apologize. The difficulty of any peaceful solution was increased by the stiffness and exaggerated dignity of communication required by the dueling code. In fact, Dr. Merryman and General Whiteside did not agree later about the details of what took place at this time; each subsequently published his own version of what occurred, fell out over the differences in their stories, and prepared to fight a duel themselves! By that time dueling was threatening to become an epidemic in Springfield.

Arrangements moved forward in a tangled fashion with the result that on Thursday, September 22, 1842, two groups of grim-faced men repaired by boat to the chosen dueling ground, "Bloody Island," about three miles from Alton, Illinois, but on the Missouri side of the Mississippi River. They thus removed themselves from the jurisdiction of the State of Illinois into a state whose laws did not forbid dueling. Lincoln's party included Dr. Merryman, William Butler, Albert T. Bledsoe (another good friend), and the devoted Dr. Henry, who, by his own account later, hoped he could help make peace. This party arrived first and when Shields and Whiteside appeared, they found Mr. Lincoln engaged in clearing away the underbrush which covered the ground.

Various recollections describing the scene at Bloody Island have been handed down. One account tells how Shields, after the clearing was made, solemnly sat down on a fallen log at one side of it and Lincoln sat down on a log opposite, while the seconds busily marked off the lines of the dueling space. Instead of the "plank ten feet long, & from nine to twelve inches broad to be firmly fixed on edge" which Lincoln's duel instructions had specified, they prepared and used a pole set in the crotches of two forked stakes. This done, the seconds soberly passed notes back and forth.

Shields's doctor, who was opposed to the duel, argued until he lost patience and angrily threatened to chastise the stubborn Irishman. At one point Lincoln stood up and, raising his great sword toward a tree, clipped off a twig at an almost unbelievable height above him, thus giving a graphic demonstration of the distance attained when his length of arm was added to that of the sword.

Meanwhile the news of the impending duel had reached Mary's cousin John J. Hardin, who had been away from Springfield attending court in another town. He, with another mutual friend of both principals, hurried to Bloody Island with the purpose of reconciling the antagonists. According to a newspaper account written many years later, Mr. Hardin told the two men they were "both d——d fools" and made some other salutary remarks as to the ridiculousness of the whole affair. Mary later gave her cousin credit for effecting the reconciliation. At all events, with all these resourceful men doing their best to prevent the fight, somehow the matter was adjusted. Without Shields's knowledge his friends withdrew his first note, whereupon Lincoln's friends read his apology. The seconds did not agree afterwards as to which of the two principals gave in first. Peace was restored and the parties embarked to return to Alton.

American humor is irrepressible. The story goes that a practical joker was on board. As the craft approached Alton the anxious spectators on the bank were horrified to see a figure lying in the boat covered with blood while another figure bent over it vigorously plying a fan. Not until the boat was quite close could it be seen that the prone figure was a log of wood and the "blood" a red flannel shirt. The practical joker dropped his fan, stood up, and grinned delightedly at the expression on the faces of those who had been taken in.

But the dueling affair was one that Lincoln could never joke about. It remained the most humiliating experience of his life. He could never endure to have the subject mentioned. He "was always so ashamed of it," wrote Mary later, that "we mutually agreed — never to speak of it ourselves." It was not safe for anyone else to speak of it either. Mary told of an incident which happened late in the Lincoln Presidency. She and her husband were standing together talking to their guests in the drawing room of the White House when an officer said playfully to Lincoln: "Mr. President, is it true, as I have heard that you, once went out, to fight a duel & all for the sake of the lady by your side." Mr. Lincoln, his face flushed painfully, replied: "I do not deny it, but if you desire my friendship, you will never mention it again."

Mary herself did not enjoy thinking back to what she described as "the foolish and uncalled for rencontre, with Gen Shields." It was, she said, "so silly" and a "very unnecessary episode." There was a hint of wifely apology in her account of Mr. Lincoln's accepting the challenge and going to Bloody Island: she said he did it "scarcely knowing what he was doing." It was an understanding and charitable comment; the whole situation had been strange and unprecedented to the man who had grown up in a log cabin and had to learn belatedly the standards and customs of more sophisticated environments. Out of the episode he came to realize the unfairness of anonymous ridicule and the wisdom of balanced consideration before taking action. He was not to forget these lessons.

It is pleasant to record that neither Mary nor Abraham cherished any resentment toward Mr. Shields. On January 1, 1862, as President and Mrs. Lincoln stood in the great

East Room of the White House receiving the long line of guests at their New Year's reception, there appeared before them the same James Shields (now a General) who more than nineteen years before had gone to Bloody Island to fight lawyer Lincoln. The presidential pair greeted him with unusual graciousness and cordiality and made him the object of their special attention.

Mr. Lincoln wrote to Joshua on October 5 to inform him "that the duelling business still rages in this city. Day-before-yesterday Shields challenged Butler, who accepted. . . ." Arrangements, however, proved difficult and they called it off because of the law. "Thus ended, duel No. 2," continued Mr. Lincoln, but "yesterday," Whiteside "chose to consider himself insulted by Dr. Merryman, and so, sent him a kind of *quasi* challenge. . . ." Dr. Merryman made Lincoln his representative and now the roles were reversed: Lincoln had to carry notes back and forth while the former seconds of his duel tied themselves up in knots trying to make arrangements for theirs. The matter was still unsettled, wrote Lincoln, "while the town is in a ferment and a street fight somewhat anticipated." The Whiteside-Merryman duel, like No. 2, failed to eventuate and one can at last abandon this much ado about duels without actual bloodshed.

Telling Joshua about the dueling business was not the main purpose of Lincoln's letter to his friend at this time; he wanted to ask Speed, a married man of nearly eight months' standing, an important question: how did he feel about his marriage now? How that marriage turned out, incidentally, is an interesting matter. One cannot possibly leave Mr. and Mrs. Speed without knowing whether all those agonizing doubts proved in the end to be what Lincoln finally called them: "all the worst sort of nonsense."

A complete and moving answer is found in a letter which Joshua sent to Fanny of the "heavenly *black eyes*" after they had been married many years: "I wrote to you yesterday, and to-day, having some leisure, I will write again upon the principle, I suppose, that where your treasure is there will your heart go. My earthly treasure is in you; not like the treasures only valuable in possession; not like other valuables acquiring increased value from increased quantity; but, satisfied with each other, we will go down the hill of life together as we have risen."

So they lived happily ever after in the fair land of Kentucky.

CHAPTER 18

"Matter of Profound Wonder"

A N ordeal shared by two lovers is apt to make clearer to each the genuineness and depth of feeling of the other. The intense emotions of those six days when the duel was threatening had drawn Mary and Abraham even closer together. This thing of seeing each other only at a few secret meetings could not go on forever; the ultimate purpose of getting engaged was to get married.

There were many plans and decisions to make. Where should they live? Where should the wedding take place? They had to face the fact that Elizabeth Edwards was going to be up in arms when she learned that, in spite of all her efforts to the contrary, her younger sister was going to marry, as she thought, beneath her.

At what time these problems were worked out between the two is not clear. It may have seemed providential to them that the sister of Mary's cousin John J. Hardin (the one who had rendered such good service at the dueling ground) was to be married in Jacksonville on September 27. If they both attended the wedding of Martinette Hardin, what opportunities the trip would afford for stolen moments of being alone with each other when they could give expression to their affection and talk about future plans!

It is said that they attended that marriage and doubtless never before had the words of the wedding ceremony seemed so beautiful and full of meaning. It is an emotional experience for an engaged couple to witness the joining together of two other young people "in holy matrimony." It usually works as a stimulus.

Mary may have felt some bitterness that the opposition of her family made it impossible for her to plan her wedding with her sisters in the usual way, making it the occasion of rejoicing, feasting, and merriment. She would have loved such preparations down to the least detail of dress, decoration, and wedding cake. Elizabeth Edwards had given their sister Frances an elaborate wedding when she married Dr. Wallace; it had been quite an affair and Frances had worn a white satin wedding gown. But she, Mary, must wear whatever she had and be married without any festive trimmings.

It is to be hoped that they were able to make some of their plans on the Jacksonville trip, because Mr. Lincoln had to be out of town on the judicial circuit much of October. It was early in that month he had written his letter to Joshua, telling incidentally of the dueling fever, but mainly to ask an important question. Apparently having a last mild qualm of doubt and reluctance to give up his bachelorhood, Abraham wanted a final boost of encouragement from Joshua the married man. Mr. Lincoln wrote that he knew his friend was happier now than when he was first married nearly eight months before, because Joshua had told him so. "But I want to ask a closer question — " he continued. " 'Are you now, in *feeling* as well as *judgement,* glad you are married as you are?' From any body but me, this would be an impudent question not to be tolerated; but I know you will pardon it in me. Please answer it quickly as I feel impatient to know." Joshua doubtless answered this appeal with the proper reassurance.

Mary and Abraham worked out their plans. They would board for a while and live in one room because it was cheaper. They could get room and board at the Globe Tavern for only four dollars a week. It was conveniently located about a block and a half from the public square. Such living would be quite a comedown for Mary after being at one of the most aristocratic homes in Springfield, but she was not afraid of that. She would face poverty and hard work cheerfully and they would improve their condition together. With his brains and big heart Mr. Lincoln was going to be a great man some day.

What minister should they ask to marry them? Since coming to make her home in Springfield Mary had been attending the Episcopal church to which her sister Elizabeth belonged, but in Lexington she had grown up a Presbyterian like her Scottish ancestors. Mr. Lincoln did not belong to any church, but he was always friendly to and cooperative with the ministers of the town and was well liked by them. The couple decided to ask Dr. Charles Dresser, the Episcopal minister, who lived in a story-and-a-half brown cottage at the corner of Eighth and Jackson Streets. (They did not know then they would buy that house and spend in it the happiest years of their lives.)

As to the place, perhaps the simplest way would be to go to Dr. Dresser's house and have the ceremony performed there. One presumes that those loyal friends Simeon Francis and his wife would gladly have offered the home which had sheltered the secret meetings, but most accounts agree that they planned to be married at the minister's.

At some point Mary and Abraham must have had a conference on a matter of deep sentiment: what should be engraved in the wedding ring? Perhaps at the same time the measurement for that ring was taken. Mary had lovely hands, small and white; her quick, pretty gestures with them were a part of her personality. It is always a tender occasion when the prospective bridegroom takes the measurement of the finger which is to wear his wedding ring.

One imagines them talking over that inscription together, considering this or that tender phrase, and finally making their decision. It was a choice which reflected the attitude of both in this fundamental step they were about to take. Lincoln's attitude toward marriage, with his concept of its sacred obligations, has been seen. He was scrupulously truthful and careful that his words should always express his exact meaning. It was said of him that he would not use the conventional greeting "I am delighted to see you" unless he meant it literally.

Both prospective bride and groom were approaching this union with an earnestness and depth of feeling that had overridden obstacles that would have blocked a less genuine attachment. That they felt their love was sacred and lasting is suggested by the words they selected to be engraved in that small gold circle: "Love is eternal."

Mr. Lincoln paid a visit to Chatterton's jewelry shop,

which he had passed so often, as it was close to Joshua's old store on the west side of the square. The ring was bought and instructions given, doubtless with a caution as to secrecy, for the inscription and date to be engraved therein. That date was November 4, 1842. It came on a Friday, and when it dawned, the plans of Mary and Abraham were complete.

Early that morning Mary announced to her sister Elizabeth that she was going to marry Mr. Lincoln that day. Storm broke out in the Edwards mansion on the hill. One suspects that Elizabeth was not only somewhat inclined to believe in the divine right of the Todds, she was perhaps touched also with a belief in the divine right of eldest sisters. She protested, scolded, gave dire warnings. How could she let her headstrong younger sister ruin her life by marrying a plebeian? "Do not forget that you are a Todd," she cried vehemently. Mary stood her ground and could be trusted to give back words as hot as those she received. The eyes of the two sisters undoubtedly flashed, while stinging retorts went back and forth.

But Mary and Mr. Lincoln had made their plans so well, with complete independence of the Edwardses, that Elizabeth found she was powerless to stop the marriage. At the end of the quarrel the firm fact remained that Mary was going to marry Mr. Lincoln that very day.

Meanwhile that gentleman had dropped around to the brown house on Eighth Street, where he found the Dresser family still at breakfast. "I want to get hitched tonight," he told the minister. That arrangement completed, he met Ninian Edwards on the street and announced to him that he and Mary were to be married that evening. Ninian made the decision that since Mary was his ward she must be married at his house. Here Ninian was siding with Lincoln, giving his consent as guardian to the marriage, and in that sense helping him "get his wife."

Elizabeth, defeated as to stopping the marriage, was further upset by that. How could she, model housekeeper and correct hostess that she was, prepare a suitable marriage feast on such short notice? How could she bake a wedding cake in time? There was only one bakery in Springfield — Dickey's — and the best that it could offer was gingerbread and beer. Elizabeth needled her sister by remarking: "I guess I will have to send to old Dickey's for some of his gingerbread and beer." Mary, stung by the terms used in the quarrel, flashed back hotly: "Well, that will be good enough for plebeians, I suppose."

But Ninian's opinion prevailed and in the end it was determined that for the sake of appearances and propriety the wedding should take place in the Edwards home. This decision was not agreed to without some discussion; too much indignation had been aroused by the conflict of that morning, which was a culmination of those months of talking Mr. Lincoln down, months when he could not even come to the house. Probably Mary finally agreed because she so loved festivities. It would be wonderful to have a real wedding after all, with guests and a wedding cake. One suspects the decision was not to Mr. Lincoln's liking: he could hardly feel comfortable in the home from which he had been frozen out so long. This thing of getting married was a nervous enough business without having one's prospective sister-in-law looking on with tight-lipped disapproval.

Once the decision to have the wedding at the Edwardses' was made, feverish activity commenced. Friends must be invited, Mary must do some last-minute shopping (trust her for that), the wedding cake and other refreshments must be prepared. She must ask several of her friends to be bridesmaids. Mr. Lincoln was to drop in and ask Mr. Matheny to be his best man; how he must have longed for Joshua instead!

"Cousin Lizzie" Todd, looking out of the window of her father's home that day, was surprised to see Mary running down the street with the air of one who has important news. Arriving breathless, Mary exclaimed: "Oh Elizabeth, I'm going to be married tonight to Mr. Lincoln and I want you to stand up with me!" Elizabeth made the eternally feminine answer: "I've nothing to wear." Mary, having already overcome seemingly immovable obstacles, brushed that off with: "You must get something." The two girls decided that Elizabeth's best white dress would do after she had washed and ironed it.

It is said that Mary asked Elizabeth's father, her uncle, Dr. John Todd, to go and break the news to her sister Frances Wallace. Without the use of telephones and with time so short, a sort of relay system of notifying the relatives was almost necessary. Dr. Todd received the news calmly and was helpful. In fact, the men of the family seem to have accepted the marriage, now that it was inevitable, more philosophically than the women. Frances was notified and hurried to the Edwards home to help with the household preparations. Someone by that time had doubtless looked up the recipe for wedding cake and the wedding supper was prepared in frantic haste.

It is impossible to tell exactly what Mary wore as a bride. All the details of the wedding day must be taken from recollections told long after the event and recollections are as fallible as human nature itself. One is variously informed that the bride wore "one of her lovely embroidered white muslin dresses," a "dress of white satin," and one made of "delaine, or something of that kind." Nobody knew that a future President of the United States was being married that night and wrote down such details at the time; it was only lawyer Lincoln and Molly Todd and weddings like that were taking place in Springfield all the time.

But it is certain that the girl who so loved beautiful clothes and was always careful to set off her daintiness according to the latest style print from *Godey's Lady's Book* took pains to dress herself prettily for her wedding. If one, by a sort of time machine, could be taken back to that November evening in the year 1842 and see her when she, after giving a last adjusting touch to the shining chestnut hair, was ready to emerge from her maiden chamber, one's heart would go out to her as it does to a bride in any generation. Imagination pictures the full skirt, the drawn-in curve of the girlish waist, a dainty bodice, and above it the vivid face with its rare coloring tremulous with emotion.

In getting dressed, Mary probably had help from some of the other girls. At least the groom had assistance in the matter and undoubtedly needed it. Mr. Lincoln in his room at the William Butler home was struggling with the final details of arraying himself in apparel appropriate for a groom, when the motherly Mrs. Butler, already attired in her best party dress, walked down the hall to tie his tie for him. She well knew he would never get it tied properly himself. A couple of the children followed her but found Mr. Lincoln was not in the mood for banter and romping. He was probably at that moment more convinced than ever that he had "defective nerves." Nervousness at this stage is normal for bridegrooms and he had to face the battery of Mary's relatives instead of going quietly to Dr. Dresser's.

A line of hastily invited guests had climbed the hill to the Edwards mansion; now they were assembled in the parlor, about thirty in all. The long dining table, whose cover had a turtledove design deemed very appropriate for such occasions, stood ready for the wedding supper. Feminine industry and culinary skill had triumphed: the wedding cake was ready. But it had been a close thing and when it was placed before the guests, the cake was still warm from the baking.

The audience ceased its rustling as the wedding party formed the tableau: Dr. Dresser in ministerial robes standing in front of the fireplace, his prayer book lighted by the two oil lamps on the mantel, the bride and groom facing him, best man and bridesmaids grouped around. The eyes of the onlookers noted handsome "Cousin Lizzie" in her freshly ironed white dress, pretty, brown-eyed Anna Rodney, and Julia Jayne, who had had a part in Mary's "Rebecca" letter.

The main attention was naturally focused on the back view of the two central figures, the tall lank man with dark

hair doubtless a little shaggy and out of control as usual,
the pretty form of the girl who looked so amusingly short
by contrast as she stood beside him, her bright head uplifted. Perhaps guests standing to the side could get a
glimpse of her piquant profile with its pleasing tilt of nose.

In the hush that fell as the minister prepared to speak,
rain could be heard beating against the windows. Dr.
Dresser gave the opening lines of the Episcopal marriage
service: "Dearly beloved, we are gathered together here in
the sight of God, and in the face of this company, to join
together this Man and this Woman in holy Matrimony. . . ."

The minister's voice went on with the words of the ceremony. He joined their right hands, that of the woman, so
small and white, almost lost in the mighty fist that had
wielded an ax in the forest.

The voice that was to speak immortal words at Gettys-
burg repeated after the minister: "I Abraham take thee
Mary to my wedded Wife, to have and to hold from this
day forward, for better for worse, for richer for poorer, in
sickness and in health, to love and to cherish, till death us do
part . . . and thereto I plight thee my troth." The girl's
soft voice repeated the vows in her turn.

Mr. Lincoln then placed the wedding ring on Mary's
finger, repeating after the minister: "With this Ring I thee
wed, and with all my worldly goods I thee endow." One of
the guests, standing close behind the bridal couple, caused
a moment's unseemly interruption here. Roughhewn Judge
Thomas Browne, who was apparently unfamiliar with this
wedding ceremony and whose mind ran more to legality

than sentiment, with a mouth-filling oath ejaculated audibly that the statute fixed all that. The voice of Dr. Dresser flickered a moment as he struggled to overcome his amusement and then resumed. The raindrops were still splashing against the windowpanes. "Forasmuch as Abraham and Mary have consented together in holy wedlock, and . . . have given and pledged their troth . . . I pronounce that they are Man and Wife. . . ."

Then, as always at home weddings, hushed solemnity broke suddenly into animated merriment, congratulations, and joviality. In the feasting that followed with the cutting of the wedding cake, the nervous bride is said to have spilled coffee on her bodice. Added to the usual nervousness of brides in general had been the conflict and tension in the Edwards home that day. But after all it had been a pretty and appropriate wedding.

The moment arrived for the departure of bride and groom. Mr. and Mrs. Abraham Lincoln went out from the richly illuminated scene of fine home, friends in gala attire, and gay festivity to proceed through the dark and rain to a room in an ordinary boardinghouse. Its door closed behind the two in whose ears still rang the strange, sweet words of the minister: "Man and Wife."

Each generation of young people discovers anew the marvel of marriage. A few days later Abraham Lincoln found his own simple words to express it; his marriage, he wrote, was to him "matter of profound wonder."

On the white, untouched pages of their future certain words were to be recorded which show how this couple

kept the vows which they had taken. They had been joined
"for better for worse, for richer for poorer," and life gave
them its usual mixture of all these states of being. There
were those happy years in Springfield when the children
were small, years of kind neighborliness, peaceful small-
town living, and increasing prominence for Mr. Lincoln.
They were "the happiest stages of life," wrote Mary. Then
came the pomp and circumstance of the Presidency. But it
was their lot to weep together over the still dead faces of
two little sons and to live through war and bloodshed in a
divided country. Yet always they would be united in their
troubles and their purposes: ". . . our deep & touching
sorrows," said Mary, "were *one* & the same. . . ."

"To hold . . . in sickness and in health." Mary remembered how, when their first baby was born, "my darling
husband, was bending over me, with such love and tenderness. . . ." "*He* was never himself — when I was not perfectly well," she wrote and again she mentioned his care of
her in her frequent illnesses, the "loving eyes — watching
over me . . . so filled with *his* deep love."

"To love and to cherish." "It was always," wrote Mary,
"music in my ears, both before & after our marriage, when
my husband, told me, that I was the only one, he had ever
thought of, or cared for." "I . . . fell in love with her,"
said Abraham, "and . . . I have never fallen out."

"Till death us do part." To Mary, when he was taken
from her, that was not the end. Her letters reiterate her
unwavering belief that she would see him again: ". . . the
only consolation left me, is the *certainty*, that each day
brings me nearer my 'loved & lost.'" "I shall not much

longer be separated from my idolized husband, who has only 'Gone before' and I am certain is fondly watching and waiting for our re-union, nevermore to be separated."

She had the comfort of a deep religious faith. And Mr. Lincoln had placed upon her finger a wedding ring with his promise of eternal love.

Bibliographical Note

To a large extent this book has been written from contemporary letters. Lincoln's letters are, of course, contained in *The Collected Works of Abraham Lincoln* (8 vols.), edited by Roy P. Basler with assistant editors Marion Dolores Pratt and Lloyd A. Dunlap (1953). Especially pertaining to this study are Lincoln's letters to Mary Owens, his account of his courtship of her in his letter to Mrs. Orville H. Browning, April 1, 1838, his "Rebecca" letter of August 27, 1842, his letter to James Shields on September 17, 1842, and his "Memorandum of Duel Instructions" to Elias H. Merryman two days later. Lincoln's letters to Joshua Speed in 1841 and 1842 are of supreme importance in tracing his thoughts and emotions about his courtship, and his letters to his wife in later years show the affection and unity of their marriage.

Mary Todd's letters to Mercy Levering in 1840 and 1841, which are so essential in tracing her thoughts and emotions for this period, are to be found in "The Documents" of Carl Sandburg's and Paul M. Angle's *Mary Lincoln: Wife and Widow* (1932). Her accounts of the Shields duel in her letters to Dr. J. G. Holland, December 4, 1865, and to F. B. Carpenter, December 8, 1865, are both also in "The Documents." In writing *Mary Lincoln: Biography of a Marriage*, I assembled an extensive collection of photostats of her letters during her whole life and these have been used here and there in *The Courtship.*

The original letters of those whom I call the subsidiary lovers in this story, James C. Conkling and Mercy Levering, are in the Illinois State Historical Library. Certain passages in these letters pertaining to the Lincolns are well-known, but I have dipped into their richness of human interest and period flavor for material which has not, to my knowledge, been published before.

The letters of Matilda Edwards (which I used for the first time in *Mary Lincoln: Biography of a Marriage* through the courtesy of their owner, Colonel Edwards M. Quigley) are essential to rule out the erroneous idea that Lincoln ever loved Matilda. I have used additional material from them in this book. Two letters of Mary Owens (Mrs. Mary S. Vineyard), written May 23 and July 22, 1866, to William H. Herndon, telling of Lincoln's courtship of her, are in the Herndon-Weik Manuscripts at the Library of Congress. Mary S. Owens's letter to Thomas J. Nance, Green City, Kentucky, April 11, 1835, which has come to attention somewhat recently, is published in the *Journal of the Illinois State Historical Society*, Spring 1955. The letter is in the article "New Salem Community Activities: Documentary," edited by Fern Nance Pond.

The Herndon-Weik Manuscripts also contain the statements of Mr. and Mrs. Ninian W. Edwards, Joshua Speed, and others about the Lincoln-Todd courtship which Herndon took from them after Lincoln's death. This evidence has been analyzed in *Mary Lincoln: Biography of a Marriage* to prove the falseness of some of the ideas set forth by Herndon.

The Robert Todd Lincoln Collection of the Papers of Abraham Lincoln in the Library of Congress contains the two letters relating to the attitude of Ninian W. Edwards toward the Lincoln-Todd marriage: William Yates to Lincoln, Springfield, Illinois, May 22, 1863, and Ninian W. Edwards to Lincoln, Springfield, June 18, 1863.

The following articles have been useful: "A Story of the Early Days in Springfield — And a Poem," in the *Journal of the Illinois State Historical Society*, April–July 1923 (for the dray ride); "Miss Todd Is Flourishing," *Lincoln Herald*, December 1948–February 1949 (for the gossiping letter about Lincoln and Matilda Edwards); Roy P. Basler's "The Authorship of the 'Rebecca' Letters," *Abraham Lincoln Quarterly*, June 1942; Mary Edwards Brown's "Abraham Lincoln Married 78 Years Ago Today," *Illinois State Register*, November 4, 1920; Eugenia Jones Hunt's "My Personal Recollections of Abraham and Mary Todd Lincoln," *Abraham Lincoln Quarterly*, March 1945; Octavia Roberts's "We All Knew Abr'ham," *Abraham Lincoln Quarterly*, March 1946; Mary Edwards Raymond's *Some Incidents in the Life of Mrs. Benj. S. Edwards*, privately printed pamphlet in the Illinois State Historical Library; Mrs. Frances Todd Wallace's *Lincoln's Marriage: Newspaper Interview . . . Springfield, Ill., Sept. 2, 1895*, privately printed leaflet, also in the Illinois State Historical Library.

Granddaughters of two bridesmaids at the Lincoln-Todd

wedding have personally supplied details: Mrs. Mary Grimsley Donaldson, granddaughter of Elizabeth Todd Grimsley, in interviews, and Miss Anna Cushman Glover, granddaughter of Anna Rodney Cushman, in interviews and a long letter giving a full account of her grandmother.

The *Sangamo Journal* for September 2, 9, and 16, 1842, has been used for the "Rebecca" letters and the poem signed "Cathleen." A few items have been taken from later newspapers.

Among the books used, Paul M. Angle's *"Here I Have Lived": A History of Lincoln's Springfield, 1821–1865* (1935) has been indispensable for portraying the early Springfield. Katherine Helm's *Mary, Wife of Lincoln* (1928), which contains recollections and extracts from the diary of her mother, Emilie Todd Helm, Mrs. Lincoln's half sister, has been important. *Herndon's Life of Lincoln*, edited by Paul M. Angle (1942), Harry E. Pratt's *Lincoln, 1809–1839* (1941) and Lincoln, *1840–1846* (1939), both giving the day-by-day activities of Lincoln, and William H. Townsend's *Lincoln and His Wife's Home Town* (1929) have all given valuable material. Mr. Townsend's larger and more recent volume, *Lincoln and the Bluegrass* (1955), also contains the material used from *Lincoln and His Wife's Home Town*. Joshua Fry Speed's *Reminiscences of Abraham Lincoln and Notes of a Visit to California* (1884) contains his letter to his wife in later life. Dr. Anson G. Henry's account of the Lincoln-Shields duel is in Francis B. Carpenter's *The Inner Life of Abraham Lincoln: Six Months at the White House* (1883). Elizabeth Keckley's *Behind the*

Scenes (1868), Ward Hill Lamon's *Recollections of Abraham Lincoln*, edited by Dorothy Lamon Teillard (1895), and Henry C. Whitney's *Life on the Circuit with Lincoln*, edited by Paul M. Angle (1940), have all contributed sidelights.